GW00370813

A taste of the North East

First published 2005
by ncjMedia Ltd
Groat Market,
Newcastle upon Tyne, NE1 1ED
ISBN 978-0-9552360-4-4

Editors: Jane Hall
Design team: Ian Guy, Sarah Mullaney, Kevin Waddell

Printed by Journal Print Media Ltd

A taste of the North East

Photography by Tony Hall | Lewis Arnold

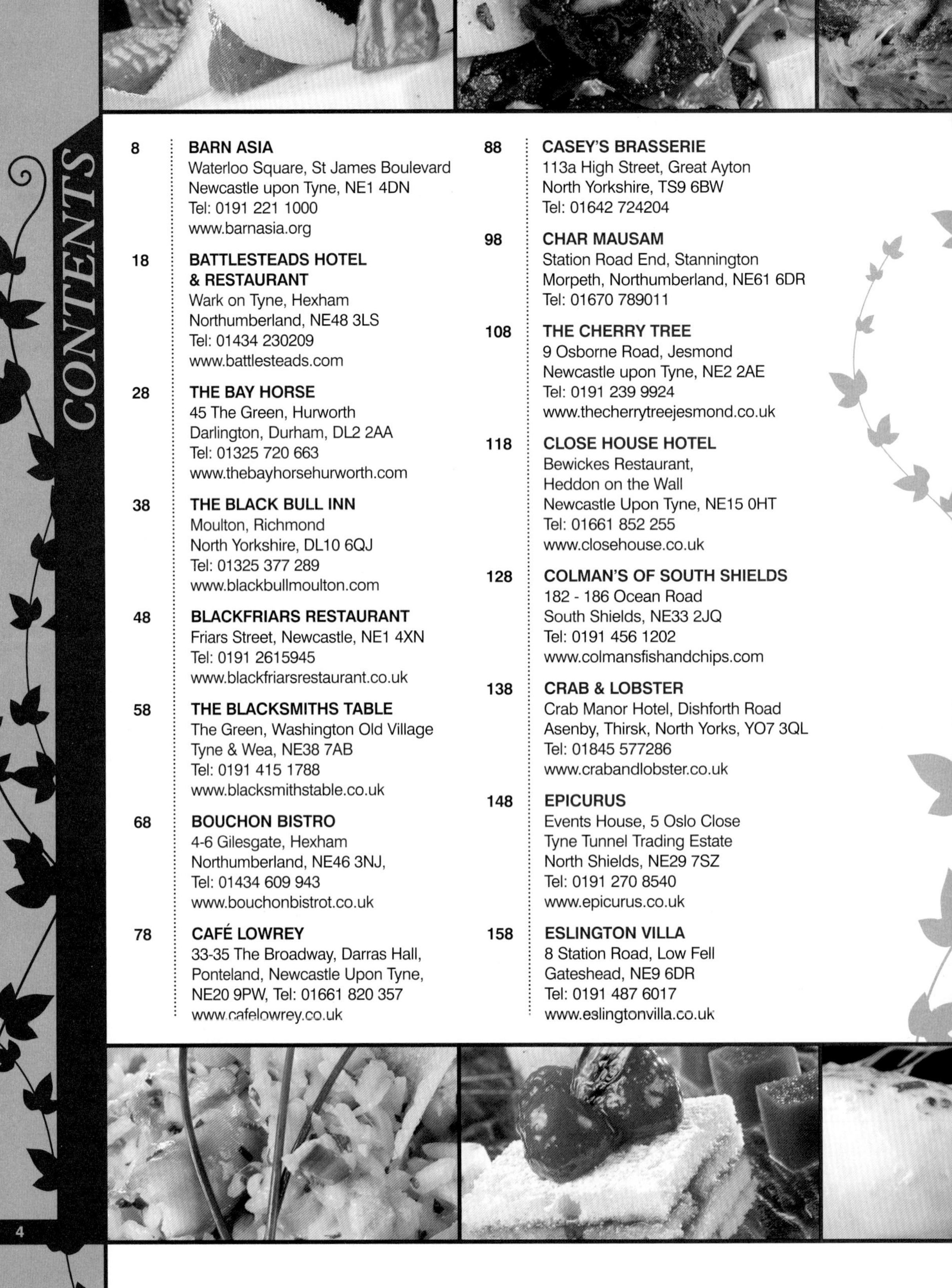

CONTENTS

CONTENTS

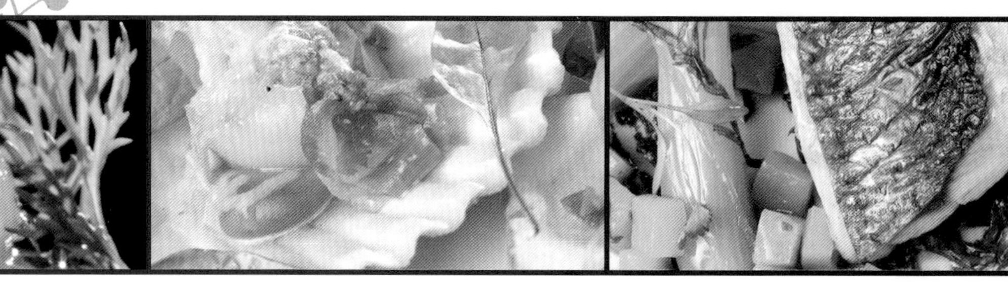

Brian Aitken
Journal editor

A TASTE OF THE NORTH EAST DOES EXACTLY WHAT IT SAYS ON THE COVER

IT IS a 320-page book of seriously delicious but diversely different recipes from the region's top chefs and restaurateurs that all share one common denominator: they each champion the finest North East produce. The North East was once cruelly derided as a culinary desert, with nothing to offer the serious food lover in the way of either quality produce or fine dining.

Nothing could now be further from the truth. From Michelin-starred restaurants to award-winning gastro pubs, county house hotels and even fish and chip shops - South Shields is home to the best in the UK as judged by celebrity chefs Gary Rhodes and Brian Turner - there are no shortage of fabulous places to eat out for occasional diners and serious foodies alike.

But a restaurant or chef is only as good as the ingredients they use. And those passionate about their craft choose to stay local. Low on mileage and high on taste, the North East has a head's start when it comes to food production thanks to our wonderful resources: the sea, the hills, the rivers, fantastic farm land and clean, fresh air in abundance. From the only harvested mussels between The Wash and Aberdeen to oysters grown within the nature reserve at Holy Island, award-winning heather-fed lamb, beef, game, vegetables, cheese, puddings, preserves and pies, the North East has it all.

All this wonderful food is due to the tireless dedication of our local producers, people who badly need our support and encouragement. There can be no better motivation than trying your hand at the inventive and exciting dishes served up in this, the fourth edition of A taste of the North East. We have persuaded 31 restaurants to reveal their culinary secrets with menus that will take you from family dining to celebrating with friends and romantic evenings at home.

Each recipe is accompanied by mouth-watering photographs, so there really is no excuse not to head out with the shopping basket and fill it with the wonderful array of fresh, flavoursome seasonal produce to be found at the region's farmers' markets, farm shops, butchers, bakers, traditional game dealers and quality independent retailers.

So don your apron, fuel your imagination and get cooking.

BARN ASIA

Push

GÌ QUÝ HƠN
ĐỘC LẬP TỰ DO
NOTHING IS MORE VALUABLE THAN INDEPENDENCE AND FREEDOM

BARN ASIA

The Barn restaurants have been serving the people of Newcastle for the past seventeen years. Renowned for their innovative cuisine and distinctive interior design, you always know when you are in a 'Barn.'

Their latest incarnation (and surely the most stylish yet) serves a fantastic blend of South East Asian favours including dishes from Vietnam, Cambodia and Thailand. The decor features propaganda artwork from the Vietnam war that was sourced personally by owner Mark Lagun.

Mark was accompanied by head chef Andy Drape when they travelled to Vietnam to sample the fabulous flavours first hand. As the recipient of the much coveted 2009 Remy Martin/Harden's Guide regional award they have added many new converts to their loyal following in the city.

"We hope to become more involved in the events side of the industry," explains Mark, "such as corporate events and outside catering." With a beautifully planted outdoor terrace, Barn Asia is also a superb venue for weddings and all manner of celebrations that require an establishment that's a little different.

Situated only five minutes walk from Central station, the midweek early bird menu has proved to be a big hit with visitors to the Newcastle Arena and the Tyne Theatre in turn. So if you are looking for a new restaurant experience, try Barn Asia - you won't be disappointed!

Mark Lagun, owner

Waterloo Square, St James Boulevard, Newcastle upon Tyne, NE1 4DN
Tel: 0191 221 1000, www.barnasia.org

BARN ASIA

BEEF RENDANG WITH ORGANIC CUMIN AND DILL ROTI BREADS

METHOD

For the rendang: Put one of the onions in a food processor, with the garlic and fresh ginger. Add 1-3 tablespoons of coconut milk until smooth. Marinate the beef over night in the onion mixture. Next day colour the remaining sliced onions in a hot wok and transfer to a large pan. Repeat this with the diced beef until the beef has coloured (best done in small amounts at a time). Add all of the remaining ingredients, except the lemon juice, and bring to the boil. Slowly cook the rendang for 2-3 hours stirring occasionally until tender. This can be stored in the fridge for a few days. When re-heating the rendang in a pan, stir in the lemon juice and serve with a roti bread.

For the roti bread: Combine the flour, dill and sugar in a bowl. Add the egg and cold water and knead to make a smooth dough. Divide into 6 balls on a lightly floured area and roll in to pancake shapes, sprinkling some cumin seeds on the bread (make sure they fit in the pan). Heat a frying pan with the oil and add the flat bread to the sizzling pan, this almost takes as long as a pancake. Only turn once, the roti bread will puff up as it cooks. These can be made a day in advance, but are best made fresh.

INGREDIENTS

Serves 6

RENDANG:

- 2 small onions (finely sliced)
- 2 tsp fresh ginger (coarsely chopped)
- 3 garlic cloves (lightly crushed)
- 1/2 litre coconut milk
- 1 kg diced beef (stewing or brisket is best)
- 1 tbs groundnut oil
- 1-2 tsp dried red chillies (ground)
- 2 cloves (ground)
- 1/2 cinnamon stick
- 1 tsp salt
- 1 tsp freshly ground black pepper
- 1/2 tbs ground coriander
- 1/2 tsp ground cumin
- 1/2 tsp ground ginger
- 2 tbs lemon juice

ROTI BREAD:

- 200g organic plain flour
- 1 tbs castor sugar
- 1/2 egg (lightly beaten)
- 7 tbs cold water
- 3 tbs vegetable oil
- 1 tbs cumin seeds
- 2 tbs fresh dill

Waterloo Square, St James Boulevard, Newcastle upon Tyne, NE1 4DN
Tel: 0191 221 1000, www.barnasia.org

OXTAIL AND POTATO MASAMAN CURRY

INGREDIENTS

Serves 6-8

10 long dried red chillies (de-seeded and chopped)
1 tbs grounded coriander seed
1 tsp grounded cumin seed
1 tsp grounded cinnamon
1 tsp grounded cloves
2 star anise
1 tsp ground cardamom
1 tsp ground white pepper
4 tbs chopped shallots
4 tbs chopped garlic
5 cm piece lemon grass (chopped)
1cm piece galangal (chopped)
1 tbs lime leaves (finely chopped)
1 tbs shrimp paste (roasted in foil for 10 minutes, moderate oven)
1 tbs sea salt

CURRY:

1½ kg oxtail (trimmed)
1 tsp salt
1 tbs vegetable oil
8 cardamom pods
1 litre coconut milk
6 tbs curry paste (as above)
20 small potatoes scrubbed
20 baby pickling onions
1 garlic clove, finely chopped
2 tbs tamarind water*
2 tbs lime juice
3 tbs granulated sugar
2 tbs fish sauce
6 tbs holy basil
2 tbs whole roasted peanuts (crushed slightly)

METHOD

For the paste: To make the paste blend the sea salt, chillies, coriander, cumin, cinnamon, cloves, star anise, cardamom and white pepper together in a pestle and mortar. (This can also be done in a coffee grinder) adding the rest of the ingredients, one by one, binding after each addition, until you have a smooth paste. This recipe should make about 6 tablespoons (90 ml) paste.

For the curry: In a large pan, gently warm the coconut milk until it becomes oily, then add 500ml water with the cardamom pods, now add the oxtail and simmer on low for 2 hours until the oxtail is tender. Then remove the oxtail from the coconut milk and set aside. In a wok or frying pan, heat the oil and fry the garlic until golden brown. Add the curry paste, mix well and cook for a few seconds. Add half the warmed coconut liquor and cook for a further 10 seconds, stirring all the time, until the mixture bubbles and starts to reduce. Add the oxtail and turn in the sauce to ensure that each piece is thoroughly coated. Now add the tamarind water, lime juice, sugar, fish sauce, and the remainder of the warmed coconut liquor. Simmer gently for 15 minutes, stirring from time to time. Add the potatoes and simmer for a further 4 minutes. (Depending on the size) Add the peanuts and cook for 4 minutes more. Stir in the basil last minute and pour into a serving dish and garnish with coriander and finish chilli and a few more peanuts. This dish is best served with steamed or boiled jasmine rice.

To make tamarind liquor: Pour 3 tablespoons of boiling water over the pulp and leave for 15 minutes, and then pass through a sieve.

Waterloo Square, St James Boulevard, Newcastle upon Tyne, NE1 4DN
Tel: 0191 221 1000, www.barnasia.org

POACHED STRAWBERRY AND LIME LEAF CUSTARD TRIFLE

INGREDIENTS

Serves 6-8

8 glasses (400-500cl)
8 brioche slices
½ kg fresh local strawberries

STRAWBERRY JELLY:

500ml red wine (we use an Asian Shiraz special reserve 2006)
200ml caster sugar
½ vanilla pod
1 cinnamon stick
3 gelatine sheets (soaked for about 10 minutes in cold water, until soft)

LIME LEAF CUSTARD:

8 egg yolks
75g sugar
300ml milk
300ml double cream
½ vanilla pod (seeded)
4 lime leaves

METHOD

For the strawberry jelly: Put all the ingredients in a pan except the gelatine sheets and bring to the boil. Once the wine mixture is boiling and the sugar has dissolved put to one side. Once the liquor is cool pour over the strawberries and leave over night in the fridge. Now for the first step making the trifle, at the bottom of the glass put the brioche in a neat circle, pass the strawberries through a sieve putting the liquor back on the heat to boil. Place the poached strawberries on top of the brioche. Once the gelatine sheets have softened. Add to the boiling liquor and whisk until all the sheets have dissolved. Then pass through a sieve into a jug ready to pour over the sponge. Leave to set in the fridge for 2-3 hours.

For the lime leaf custard: Whisk the egg yolks and the sugar in a large bowl, until the sugar has dissolved. Slowly heat up the milk and cream. Adding the vanilla seeds and lime leaf to the liquor, when the liquor is almost boiling, pour into the bowl with egg mixture. And whisk slightly for a few seconds. Then transfer back into the pan, stirring with a spoon at all times on a very low heat, until it coats the back of the spoon. Pick out the remaining lime leaves and leave to cool. Ready to pour over the jelly mixture. Once the custard is set just add some whipped cream (we add nutmeg through the mixture).

Waterloo Square, St James Boulevard, Newcastle upon Tyne, NE1 4DN
Tel: 0191 221 1000, www.barnasia.org

BATTLESTEADS HOTEL & RESTAURANT

Wark on Tyne, Hexham, Northumberland NE48 3LS Tel: 01434 230209, www.battlesteads.com

BATTLESTEADS
HOTEL

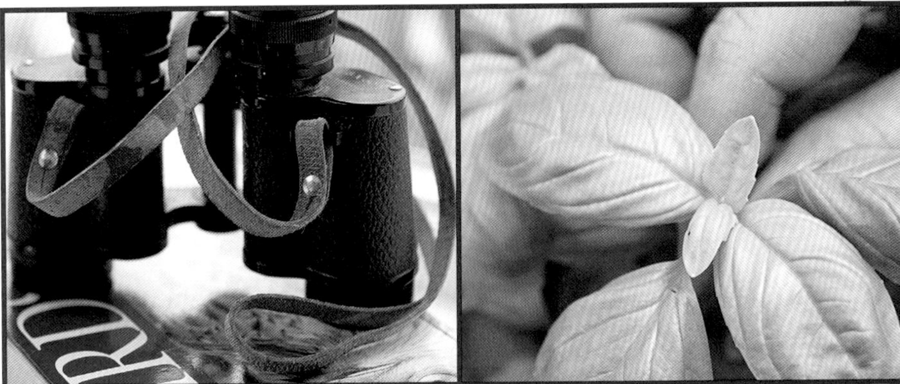

I have been Head Chef at the Battlesteads since it was bought by the owners Richard & Dee Slade in 2005.

Having worked with Richard and Dee for eight years at the very successful Magnesia Bank in North Shields, I was under no illusions as to their expectations when they asked me to head up the team at the Battlesteads.

All three of us share a passion for good quality, locally sourced food, and rural Northumberland has not disappointed us in our quest for excellence. As well as a wealth of brilliant ingredients on our doorstep we have recently constructed a polytunnel and extensive planting beds, where herbs, salads and fruits are grown for the kitchen. It has proved a real talking point among the guests and they love to see me or one of the team snipping the herbs for their plate. You can't get much fresher than that!

We thought life in the country was going to be quiet, but I'm glad to say that business is booming!

The Hotel has already won a Silver award from VisitBritain, a Gold award from the Green Tourism Business Scheme, and HRS recently awarded us Independent Winners 2009 in their Hotel Excellence Awards.

Eddie Shilton, head chef

Wark on Tyne, Hexham, Northumberland NE48 3LS
Tel: 01434 230209, www.battlesteads.com

PAN FRIED WILD RABBIT WITH LOCAL BLACK PUDDING AND APPLE

BATTLESTEADS HOTEL & RESTAURANT

METHOD

To prepare: Heat 1 tablespoon of the oil in a large frying pan. Season the rabbit and fry briskly for 1 minute, turning to brown on each side. Add the apples and fry for a further 30 seconds. Add the black pudding and fry for a further 1 minute. Whisk the remaining oil with the mustard, pour over the rocket leaves, toss lightly and divide between four plates.

To serve: Divide the rabbit mix equally between the plates, top with a few grinds of black pepper and serve with crusty bread.

INGREDIENTS

Serves 4

- 2 saddles of wild rabbit, boneless (cut into 1/2″ pieces)
- 200g good quality black pudding (cut into 1/2″ pieces)
- 2 large crisp apples (cut into 1/2″ pieces)
- 3 tbs extra virgin olive oil
- 1 tsp course grain mustard
- Salt and pepper
- 250g wild rocket
- Crusty bread to serve

Wark on Tyne, Hexham, Northumberland NE48 3LS
Tel: 01434 230209, www.battlesteads.com

BYWELL SMOKED HADDOCK WITH NORTH TYNE RARE BREED POACHED EGG, RED KING EDWARD ROSTI AND WILD GARLIC AIOLI

INGREDIENTS

Serves 4

- 4 x 200g Bywell natural smoked haddock portions
- 4 large free range eggs (we use North Tyne rare breed poultry)
- 4 large free range egg yolks (as above)
- 2 large handfuls of wild garlic (or 1/2 a bulb of garlic)
- 150ml extra virgin olive or rapeseed oil
- Salt and pepper
- 750g red King Edward potatoes (or any starchy variety)
- 1 handful of chopped chives
- Melted butter

METHOD

For the eggs: Poach four of the eggs in plenty of water with a splash of distilled vinegar until cooked to your liking, then chill in a bowl of iced water to stop them overcooking.

For the rosti: Wash, peel and par-boil the potatoes, drain and allow to cool slightly before grating them. Mix with the chopped chives and season. Brush four 3 inch round metal moulds with melted butter, fill with the rosti mix, brush with a little more melted butter and place into a pre-heated oven at 180°C for 10 minutes.

For the haddock: Bring a large deep frying pan filled with water to the boil. Poach the haddock for 5 minutes, drain and keep warm. In the same pan add the poached eggs to warm through and remove the pan from the heat.

For the aioli: Place the garlic in a food processor with the egg yolks, blitz for 1 1/2 minutes, and then slowly add the oil until it reaches a thick, creamy consistency. This can be made the day before and chilled.

To serve: Remove the rosti from the oven, cut around the outside with a knife, place onto a warm plate and remove the ring. Place the haddock on the rosti and top with a poached egg, spoon the aioli around the plate. Garnish with chopped chives or wild garlic.

Wark on Tyne, Hexham, Northumberland NE48 3LS
Tel: 01434 230209, www.battlesteads.com

DEE'S WINEMAKERS GATEAU WITH SWEET WINE SYRUP AND CRÈME FRAICHE

INGREDIENTS

Serves 12

- 2 large free range eggs
- 150g castor sugar
- 4 tbs Oleifeira virgin rapeseed oil (extra virgin olive oil is a suitable substitute)
- 60g unsalted butter (melted)
- 5 tbs whole milk
- 1/2 tsp pure vanilla extract
- 200g plain flour
- 1/2 tsp baking powder
- Pinch sea salt
- Grated zest of 1 lemon
- Grated zest of 1 orange
- 300g fresh seedless flame grapes (pink colour)
- Butter and flour for preparing the cake tin
- 100ml sweet white wine (eg Muscat)
- 300g sugar
- 500ml water
- 1/2 vanilla pod
- Crème fraiche
- Icing sugar (for decoration)

METHOD

To prepare: Preheat the oven to 180˚C and prepare a 23cm spring form cake tin with butter and flour.

For the gateau: Using an electric mixer beat the eggs and sugar until thick and creamy. Add the oil, melted butter, milk and vanilla extract and mix until blended. Sift the flour, baking powder and salt into a large bowl, add the lemon and orange zest and toss to coat. Stir the flour mixture into the egg mixture until well blended. Set aside for 10 minutes to allow the flour to absorb the liquids. Stir 3/4 of the grapes into the mixture then spoon into the cake tin. Place in the centre of the oven and bake for 15 minutes. Remove the tin from the oven and randomly sprinkle the top with the remaining grapes. Return to the oven and bake for a further 40 minutes until golden brown. Allow to cool for 10 minutes then run a knife around the sides of the tin to release the gateau.

For the syrup: Put the sugar, water and vanilla pod in a pan and bring to the boil for approximately 10 minutes until it thickens and is a straw colour. Add the sweet white wine to the sugar and reduce gently by a third, or is a thin syrup.

To serve: Serve a wedge of the gateau warm or at room temperature in a pool of wine syrup with crème fraiche, and sprinkle with icing sugar for decoration.

Wark on Tyne, Hexham, Northumberland NE48 3LS
Tel: 01434 230209, www.battlesteads.com

THE BAY HORSE

45 The Green, Hurworth, Darlington, Durham DL2 2AA , Tel: 01325 720 663, www.thebayhorsehurworth.com

The
BAY
HORSE

Set in the picturesque village of Hurworth, near Darlington, the grade two listed Bay Horse coach house dates back to the 1400's. It was extensively refurbished in October 2008 by proprietors Marcus Bennett and Jonathan Hall. Marcus and Jonathan bring with them a wealth of experience, Marcus residing as head chef, and Jonathan overseeing front of house.

The Bay Horse retains an emphasis on the finer details of a real old English pub, hand pulled local ales in dimpled pint glasses, side dishes served in copper pans, the open log fire in the main bar. All furnishings were carefully sourced from antique fayres around the country, including a late Victorian dining tables which is proudly prominent in the private dining rooms, with an adjoining ambient and cosy snug area.

The restaurant menu is made up of classic British cooking with a twist, Marcus has a strong emphasis on flavours and presentation , sourcing local produce wherever possible to make the most of the seasonal ingredients available. The dessert menu contains an expression of classical favourites, with a selection of home-made ice creams and sorbets.

In addition, a selection of bread is baked daily. The Bay Horse also boasts a lush, fully walled garden with a covered pergola area, perfect for dining in the summer months.

Marcus Bennett and Jonathan Hall, owners

45 The Green, Hurworth, Darlington, Durham DL2 2AA
Tel: 01325 720 663, www.thebayhorsehurworth.com

POTTED WHITE CRAB WITH SMOKED SALMON ROULADE, CREAMY SCRAMBLED EGG AND A BROWN CRAB DRESSING

INGREDIENTS

Serves 4

POTTED CRAB:

- 6 egg yolks
- 1 tbs Dijon mustard
- 2 tbs white wine vinegar
- Juice of 1 lemon
- 1 pt grape seed oil
- 1/2 pt olive oil
- 1/2 tsp salt
- 12tsp dry sherry
- 3 bannana shallots (finely diced)
- 1/2 tsp cayenne pepper
- 1/4 tsp grated nutmeg
- 8 tsp Worcestershire sauce
- 100g chives (finely chopped)
- 900g white and brown crab meat
- 50g melted butter

BROWN CRAB DRESSING:

- 150g brown crab meat
- 1 tsp tomato ketchup
- 1 tsp Worcestershire sauce
- 2 tsp English mustard
- Juice of 1/2 lemon
- 50ml vegetable oil
- 50ml olive oil

METHOD

For the potted crab: Place the egg yolks, Dijon mustard, salt, sherry, Worcestershire sauce, nutmeg, cayenne pepper and lemon in an electric mixer and whisk until pale and fluffy. Mix the two oils together and slowly add to the egg mixture in a thin trickle, whisking all the time. Fold in the shallots, chives and crab meat, place the crab mixture into small pots and top with melted butter and chill before serving.

For the brown crab dressing: Blend the tomato ketchup, Worcestershire sauce, crab meat and mustard until smooth. Leaving the blender on slowly pour the lemon juice into the mixture then slowly add both oils until completely binded, on a low speed.

Serve with: Smoked salmon roulade and creamy scrambled eggs.

45 The Green, Hurworth, Darlington, Durham DL2 2AA
Tel: 01325 720 663, www.thebayhorsehurworth.com

PRESSED BELLY PORK WITH ENGLISH BLACK PUDDING AND ROASTED ASPARAGUS, WHITE OYSTER MUSHROOMS AND A MADEIRA JUS

INGREDIENTS

Serves 4

BELLY PORK:

- 2kg belly pork
- $1\frac{1}{2}$ litre of chicken stock
- 1 bulb of garlic (chopped)
- 2 carrots (chopped)
- 2 sprigs of thyme
- 100g butter
- Madeira

RHUBARB CHUTNEY:

- 500g rhubarb (chopped)
- 1 star anise
- 200ml white wine vinegar
- 100ml grenadine
- 1 vanilla pod
- 1 cinnamon stick
- 1 onion (finely diced)
- 150g apple (peeled, cored and diced)

METHOD

For the belly pork: Place the belly pork skin side down in a large baking tray and spinkle with the vegetables and herbs, pour over the chicken stock and cover with tin foil. Slowly cook at 150°C for 5 hours. Remove from the oven and lift out of the stock, take out all of the bones and press between 2 baking sheets overnight in the fridge. Keep the stock to one side. To finish, cut into 6cm by 4cm portions and fry skin side down for 5 minutes then place in a 190°C oven for 10 minutes. Sieve the stock and reduce in a pan by half, whisk in 100g of butter and add a splash of Madeira before serving.

For the rhubarb chutney: Reduce the grenadine and white wine vinegar to a syrupy consistency, add the onion and cook until soft. Add the rhubarb, apple, star anise, vanilla and cinnamon and cook to a jammy consistency.

Serve the pork: With the chutney, black pudding, roasted asparagus and white oyster mushrooms, pour over the Madeira jus.

45 The Green, Hurworth, Darlington, Durham DL2 2AA
Tel: 01325 720 663, www.thebayhorsehurworth.com

VANILLA CHEESECAKE WITH POACHED STRAWBERRIES

METHOD

For the base: Combine all of the ingredients and press into a 6 inch baking tray lined with greaseproof paper and place in the fridge to set.

For the topping: Whisk the ingredients for the topping together and pour on to the set base and bake at 110˚C for 80 minutes until set.

For the strawberries: Halve or quarter the strawberries depending on size and place in a large bowl. Put the sugar and water in a large pan and slowly bring to the boil to dissolve the sugar, then add the vanilla pod and seeds and crushed peppercorns. Remove from the heat and pour the syrup over the strawberries. Leave to marinate in a warm place for 15 minutes.

Serve a slice of the cheesecake: With the poached strawberries, along with a strawberry coulis and white balsamic ice cream.

INGREDIENTS

Serves 8

CHEESECAKE BASE:

70g butter (melted)
70g ground almonds
70g ground pecan nuts
70g digestive biscuits (crushed)

CHEESECAKE TOPPING:

200g mascarpone cheese
650g cream cheese
200g sugar
1 vanilla pod
8 egg yolks
2 whole eggs

POACHED STRAWBERRIES:

500g strawberries (hulled)
100g caster sugar
100ml water
1 vanilla pod (split and seeds scraped)
4 black peppercorns (crushed)

45 The Green, Hurworth, Darlington, Durham DL2 2AA
Tel: 01325 720 663, www.thebayhorsehurworth.com

BLACK BULL INN

Moulton, Richmond, North Yorkshire DL10 6QJ, Tel: 01325 377 289, www.blackbullmoulton.com

While some restaurants follow fads and trip themselves up trying to set trends, Black Bull Inn has had the strength of character to stay true to its Anglo-French roots for over 40 years. The result is a loyal following of passionate, food loving regulars that grows with each new visitor. The location, off Scotch Corner, attracts locals dropping in for their regular treat, tourists glad to add this wonderful pit-stop to their itinerary, or gourmets making the pilgrimage to this much-respected restaurant.

Black Bull Inn is famously well regarded as a great place for seafood, due in part to the presence of their on-site salt water tanks allowing the kitchen to stock live lobsters, prawns and oysters. Our kitchen team, with Adrian Knowles – at the helm, effortlessly turn out beautifully created seasonal dishes using the finest produce, under the expert guidance of consultant chef, Jeff Baker from the highly acclaimed J Baker's Bistro Moderne, York.

The overall ambience of the Black Bull Inn is at its heart a genuine, traditional English pub with the whole offering abound with traditional charm, combined with a classic sense of luxury. Part of its character is the weathered timber beams, whitewashed walls and antiques and curios adorning the walls and shelves, with nooks and cubby-holes spurring off at every turn, and intimate private rooms and 'Hazel' the first class Pullman carriage interconnecting to the main restaurant space. Black Bull Inn has some very exciting expansion plans afoot, which include luxurious accommodation for visiting guests.

Adrian Knowles, head chef

Moulton, Richmond, North Yorkshire DL10 6QJ
Tel: 01325 377 289, www.blackbullmoulton.com

HOT & CRUNCHY OYSTERS WITH LEMON & WHITBY CRAB MAYONNAISE

METHOD

For the oysters: In three separate bowls place the egg beaten with the milk, the flour with the salt and pepper to season and the panko breadcrumbs. Dredge the oysters one at a time in the flour, then dip into the egg mix and then coat in the panko crumb. Deep fry for 30 seconds to 1 minute at 185°C in sunflower oil, until golden.

For the mayonnaise: Place the mayonnaise in a bowl, add the shallots, dill, zest & juice of the lemon and mix together. Add the crabmeat and fold through. Season to taste.

To serve: Arrange the oyster shells around a large plate or platter, place an oyster in each shell and a pot of lemon and crab mayonnaise in the centre.

INGREDIENTS

Serves 2

OYSTERS:

- 12 oysters (shucked, bottom shells washed & dried)
- 100g plain flour
- Salt and freshly milled black pepper
- 3 free range eggs
- 2 tbs milk
- 200g panko breadcrumbs (available from specialist retailers)

MAYONNAISE:

- 3 tbs organic mayonnaise
- 1 tsp shallot (finely diced)
- 1/2 tsp dill (freshly chopped)
- 1 lemon (juiced and zest finely grated)
- 50g white Whitby crab meat
- Salt and black pepper

Moulton, Richmond, North Yorkshire DL10 6QJ
Tel: 01325 377 289, www.blackbullmoulton.com

CHATEAUBRIAND, DUCK FAT VEGETABLES & SAUCE BORDELAISE

INGREDIENTS

Serves 2

CHATEAUBRIAND:

- 500g rump of beef fillet (Chateaubriand)
- 3 tbs duck fat
- Salt & freshly milled ground pepper

VEGETABLES:

- 6 small potatoes (peeled)
- 8 young carrots (ends trimmed)
- 2 sticks celery (trimmed and cut in half)
- 2 small red onions (peeled)
- 1 bunch watercress (to garnish)
- 1 tbs duck fat
- 3 cloves of garlic
- 3 sprigs of thyme
- Maldon sea salt

SAUCE:

- 2 shallots (peeled and finely diced)
- 1 clove garlic (crushed)
- 1 sprig thyme
- 1 bay leaf
- 12 peppercorns
- 2 tbs red wine vinegar
- 1 pinch sugar
- 375ml red wine (good full bodied)
- 200ml beef stock
- 50g unsalted butter (cut into ½ inch cubes)

METHOD

For the Chateaubriand: Pre heat oven to 220˚C. Heat the duck fat in a large frying pan over a high heat. Pat dry the beef fillet, season with black pepper and fry for 1-2 minutes on all sides to seal and brown. Transfer to a roasting pan and cook in the oven for up to 15 minutes until medium rare. When cooked place on a wire rack, season with salt and rest for 10-15 minutes.

For the vegetables: Reduce oven to 200˚C. Par boil the potatoes in boiling salted water for 5 minutes. Drain, then gently roast the potatoes in the duck fat for 15 - 20 minutes until tender in the centre and scatter around the rested beef. For the carrots, take a sheet of tin foil and place the carrots in the centre, add 1 tsp duck fat, 1 sprig of thyme, 1 clove of garlic and a pinch of salt. Fold up into an airtight parcel so no steam can escape. Cook on a tray in the oven at 165°C for 40 minutes until tender. Repeat this process for the onions and celery.

For the sauce: Place all of the ingredients except the red wine, beef stock and butter, into a pan and reduce down on a high heat until all the liquid has almost gone. Add the red wine and reduce to a syrup. Finally add the beef stock to the empty beef roasting tin to deglaze all of the juices then add to the pan. Reduce by a third then whisk in the unsalted butter to thicken.

To serve: On a warm plate or platter, arrange the roast vegetables and potatoes, carve the beef into four to eight slices. Garnish with watercress and serve the sauce separately.

Moulton, Richmond, North Yorkshire DL10 6QJ
Tel: 01325 377 289, www.blackbullmoulton.com

TART AU FIN

METHOD

Pre-heat the oven to 190°C: Roll out the puff pastry onto a board dusted with flour, cut out two discs of pastry 15-20cm and place on a baking sheet with greaseproof paper. Prick all over with a fork and leave to rest in the fridge.

For the frangipane: Cream together the butter and sugar until light and creamy. Add the egg, ground almonds, plain flour and milk, and fold in. Spread the frangipane over the tart base just up to the edge and smooth the top.

For the apples: Peel and core the apples, cut into 4 wedges and slice each wedge into 4-6 thin slices. Arrange the sliced apple around the tart base, working from the middle to the outside building up 2 layers. Dust with icing sugar and bake for 18-20 minutes. Make a glaze by gently heating the apricot jam and water in a saucepan. Brush over the baked tarts.

To serve: Dust with icing sugar and place a scoop of vanilla bean ice cream in the centre of each tart.

INGREDIENTS

Serves 2

1 pack (approx 250g) good quality pre-rolled puff pastry
4 Granny Smiths apples
Icing sugar (for dusting)

TO GLAZE:
2 tbs apricot jam
1/2 tbs water

FRANGIPANE:
100g unsalted butter
100g castor sugar
1 large egg (beaten)
100g ground almonds
30g plain flour
1 tbs milk

SERVE WITH:
2 scoops of vanilla bean ice cream

Moulton, Richmond, North Yorkshire DL10 6QJ
Tel: 01325 377 289, www.blackbullmoulton.com

BLACKFRIARS RESTAURANT

Friars Street, Newcastle NE1 4XN, Tel: 0191 2615945, www.blackfriarsrestaurant.co.uk

BLACKFRIARS RESTAURANT

Blackfriars Restaurant is the oldest dining room in the UK with the main restaurant originally built to house the refectory for the 'Black Friars' and as a working inner-city former monastery, it's unique. The horseshoe of buildings provides shelter for the medieval courtyard used for al fresco dining in the summer. Time-enduring and traditional, Blackfriars has long been one of the City's most recognised restaurants and is now regarded as a Newcastle institution.

Unusually, the kitchen is run completely democratically by the most dedicated, committed and enthusiastic team around. The chefs maintain everyone is equal and they all have an input into every new dish. Moreover, they continually question, re-invent and re-appraise everything they do, always moving forward, always demanding more – and all backed-up by a super - professional front of house team.

Sourcing seasonal produce from local farms and markets. The award-winning team produces gutsy traditional british menus, all accompanied by a large award-winning wine list. The main candle-lit dining room lends itself to intimate and romantic dining, with small inglenooks and hide-away corners, indeed Blackfriars was recently voted the 6th most romantic restaurant in the UK. It is also perfect for larger dining parties with the dining room split into two levels seating up to 70 diners in total.

Blackfriars has gained an AA rosette, inclusion in the Good Food Guide, Hardens and Michelin Guides.

Andy Hook, owner

Friars Street, Newcastle NE1 4XN
Tel: 0191 2615945, www.blackfriarsrestaurant.co.uk

WARM SALAD OF BRAISED COUNTY DURHAM PORK HEAD, APPLE & VANILLA PURÉE

METHOD

For the pig's head: Wash and scrub the pig's head until completely clean and soak in the chilled brine for 24 hours. Place the head in a large pan or stock pot, cover with cold water and bring to boil. Skim off any impurities that rise to the surface, add the chopped vegetables, garlic, salt, pepper and star anise. Simmer very gently for 4 hours until meat easily falls away from the bone. Remove from the cooking liquor, allow to cool before picking the meat from the bones, together with a little cheek fat to help bind. Add parsley, lemon zest and more seasoning to taste. Place 3 large sheets of cling film on a flat surface, spoon on the mixture and roll tightly to size and shape of a rolling-pin. Allow to set in fridge for 4 hours, remove, slice and pan-fry to order in butter until golden brown.

For the puree: Add the chopped apple to the pan with a splash of water and sugar, add the vanilla seeds and cook until soft. Blitz in a blender, add more sugar to taste.

To serve: Place pan-fried rolled pig's head on a plate, spoon on apple vanilla puree and garnish with wild garlic.

INGREDIENTS

Serves 4

BRINE:

10 litres water
200g salt (dissolved in water)

PIG'S HEAD:

1 Pig's head (brains removed)
1 carrot (chopped)
1 onion (chopped)
½ head of celery (chopped)
½ head of garlic
½ tsp sea salt (plus more to taste)
½ tsp white pepper corns (plus more to taste)
1 star anise
1 tbs flat leaf parsley (finely chopped)
½ lemon (zest only)
50g unsalted butter
100g wild garlic (leaves and flowers)

APPLE PUREE:

300g Bramley apples (peeled, cored and chopped)
50g sugar (plus more to taste)
½ vanilla pod (seeds scraped)

Friars Street, Newcastle NE1 4XN
Tel: 0191 2615945, www.blackfriarsrestaurant.co.uk

ROAST BARBARY DUCK BREAST, WITH HONEY SAUTÉED RADISHES

INGREDIENTS

Serves 4

- 4 Barbary duck breast
- Sea salt
- Ground black pepper
- 1 tbs olive oil
- 50 g butter
- 1kg radishes (plus leaves)
- 1 orange (juice and zest)
- 1 tsp Chainbridge honey
- 300ml beef stock

METHOD

For the duck: Set oven to 180°C. Wash the radishes and leaves in cold water, dry. Season the duck breast and place, skin-side down, in a medium hot pan for 2 minutes (no oil needed as fat will render from the meat) then turn and cook for another 2 minutes. Place in oven for 10 minutes - roast as preferred and then take out to rest.

For the radishes: Add oil and butter to hot pan and wait until butter sizzles, add radishes and sauté until tender – and pink-ish in colour. Add leaves to pan, wait till slightly wilted before adding orange zest and honey. Reduce orange juice and beef stock in separate pan.

To serve: Slice breast on diagonal into 5 pieces, place radishes and leaves in centre of plate with slice duck on top, spoon sauce over and around the duck. Serve with steamed purple sprouting broccoli or something similarly seasonal.

BLACKFRIARS RESTAURANT

Friars Street, Newcastle NE1 4XN
Tel: 0191 2615945, www.blackfriarsrestaurant.co.uk

FRIARS DARK CHOCOLATE CAKE, LINDISFARNE MEAD MARMALADE ICE CREAM

METHOD

To make chocolate cake: Cream sugars and butter together, very slowly add eggs (ensure it doesn't curdle), half the espresso and hot milk. Now add half the flour, cocoa, baking powder and bi-carbonate of soda before adding rest of espresso and milk and then all remaining ingredients. Steam in the oven four approx 1 hour.

To make ice cream: Although Blackfriars makes its own crème Anglais-based ice cream from scratch, its easier to buy a really good vanilla ice cream (there are so many good home-made ice cream makers in the North East) and stir in a chilled marmalade made by slowly stewing orange zest, sugar and mead together to a back of spoon-coating consistency.

INGREDIENTS

Makes one cake/8 slices

CHOCOLATE CAKE:

- 400g dark sugar
- 400g caster sugar
- 175g butter
- 3 eggs (beaten)
- 4 shots espresso (add half of these to mix)
- 500ml milk (heated)
- 400g flour
- 150g cocoa
- 1 tbs baking powder
- 1 tbs bi-carbonate of soda

LINDISFARNE MEAD MARMALADE ICE CREAM:

- Zest of 3 oranges
- 100g caster sugar
- 100ml Lindisfarne mead
- 400g good quality vanilla ice cream

Friars Street, Newcastle NE1 4XN
Tel: 0191 2615945, www.blackfriarsrestaurant.co.uk

THE BLACKSMITH'S TABLE

The Green, Washington Old Village, Tyne & Wear NE38 7AB, Tel: 0191 415 1788, www.blacksmithstable.co.uk

The
Blacksm 's Table
RESTAURANT

Washington Village is the most traditional of English Villages; 3 pubs, a small library, a war memorial, mature trees, a village green, an historical hall, and, on the crossroads, the village smithy. Except the smithy is no longer a smithy. Since 1988 this imposing 400 year old building has been the Blacksmith's Table, a quintessential English Restaurant in a picturesque conservation area.

Now in their 22nd year, original owner Paul Cajiao and his wife Pam have a simple mission; to provide top quality and innovative cuisine in a friendly, cosy and relaxed atmosphere,. They've never followed trends and fashions in food, other than the ones they've set themselves.

Head Chef, Mark Crook is, says Paul, "one of the most talented and experienced chefs currently working in the North East. He's been with us many years and continues to amaze us with his food knowledge and creativity. Unlike some chefs he's very approachable and willing to share his experience for the benefit of the team and the customers".

Paul and Pam's views and concepts seem to be shared by many local reviewing journalists who over the years have written many glowing accolades; "Good food prepared and cooked to perfection and an ambience all of its own, the Blacksmiths Table is a unique experience" Shields Gazette. "The Blacksmiths Table provides an eating experience par excellence, the food is delicious, the presentation first class and the service, attentive, leisurely and friendly" The Evening Chronicle. "This is one of the best restaurants in the North… if not the best "Sunderland Echo.

Paul & Pam Cajiao, owners

The Green, Washington Old Village, Tyne & Wear NE38 7AB
Tel: 0191 415 1788, www.blacksmithstable.co.uk

MIXED GAME TERRINE WITH GRENADINE ONIONS

METHOD

For the terrine: Dice all of the ingredients, and put aside. Chop the livers, mix with sausage meat and other forcemeat ingredients. Once mixed add the diced meat. Line a loaf tin or terrine with cling film. Flatten the 5 rashers of streaky bacon and line the tin / terrine. Put the mix into the tin and cover with tin foil. Bake in a tray with a little water at 160°C for approx 90 minutes. Test with knife, if it runs clear it's cooked. Place in fridge, with weight on top, leave overnight.

For the grenadine onions: Put all of the ingredients in pot without lid. Simmer until liquid is reduced. Leave to cool then serve with terrine.

INGREDIENTS

Serves 4

GAME TERRINE

- 2 pheasant breasts
- 4 pigeon breasts
- 1 duck breast (fat removed, or any other wild fowl)
- Saddle and hind quarters of hare (off the bone)
- Saddle and hind quarters of rabbit (off the bone)
- 5 rashers of streaky bacon (to line terrine)

FORCEMEAT:

- 500g sausage meat
- 250g duck livers and rabbit livers (from rabbit body)
- 2.handfulls white breadcrumbs
- 1 egg white
- 3 tbs parsley
- 3 sprigs thyme
- 6 juniper berries (crushed in pestle and mortar)
- 2 cloves garlic
- splash brandy
- splash red wine
- salt and pepper

GRENADINE ONIONS:

- 10 red onions (thinly sliced)
- 1/2 pt red wine
- 1/2 pt red wine vinegar
- 1/2 pt sweet sherry
- 1/2 pt grenadine

The Green, Washington Old Village, Tyne & Wear NE38 7AB
Tel: 0191 415 1788, www.blacksmithstable.co.uk

SMOKED COD AND SCALLOP ROULADE, LATTICED WITH LEEKS, SERVED WITH CHUNKY CHIPS AND A SALT AND VINEGAR SAUCE.

INGREDIENTS

Serves 4

ROULADE:

- 2 large leeks
- 400g smoked cod
- 8 scallops
- 2 large potatoes, cut into thick chips

SAUCE:

- 4 tbs white wine vinegar
- 4 tbs malt vinegar
- 4 tbs white wine
- 8 tbs whipping cream
- 175g salted butter
- Fresh chives

METHOD

For the lattice: Cut the leeks just under the stem at bottom then slice lengthways to top. Put in boiling water for one minute and then cool in cold water. Criss-cross the leeks to make lattice.

For the sauce: Boil the vinegars and white wine togther and reduce by half. Add the cream and butter to the wine solution, don't let it boil, and add the chives.

For the cod: Take smoked cod between 2 lengths of cling film and flatten. Remove cling film then layer onto leek lattice. Top the cod with a layer of scallops, leaving a 1inch border. Roll up and tie. Wrap in cling film then refrigerate. When required place the roulade into an oven proof dish containing hot water and white wine solution. Poach for 10 minutes, put aside to rest for 4 minutes.

To serve: Slice the roulade and serve with the sauce and chunky chips.

The Green, Washington Old Village, Tyne & Wear NE38 7AB
Tel: 0191 415 1788, www.blacksmithstable.co.uk

BEETROOT BAVAROIS WITH A CHOCOLATE CRUMBLE TOPPING

METHOD

For the crumble: Sieve the flour and cocoa togther, rub in the butter and add the sugar. When all is mixed to a crumble state, bake in oven on a flat tray. At 180°C,after 15 minutes. Break up occasionally during cooking. Let crumble cool then chop the chocolate small and mix to the crumble.

For the beetroot bavarois: Make a stock syrup by boiling togther the sugar with 8tbs water for 10 mins. Beat egg yolks to ribbon stage then beat in 50mls of stock syrup. Put gelatine in water to soften. Beat 150mls of double cream to soft peaks. Heat the remaining cream on low heat, squeeze gelatine and add. Whisk egg whites to soft peaks then slowly add rest of stock syrup (still hot). Blend the beetroot to a paste. Add to the egg yolks, then add gelatine, double cream and whisk in. Fold in the whipped cream then fold in the meringue. Set in metal ring, refrigerate for 4 hours, or until set. Top with chocolate crumble and serve with shortbread biscuit.

INGREDIENTS

Serves 6

THE CRUMBLE

- 80g plain flour
- 20g cocoa powder
- 50g butter (rub into flour and cocoa)
- 50g brown sugar
- 25g dark chocolate (70)

THE BEETROOT BAVAROIS

- 350g beetroot (boiled in packets)
- 200g caster sugar
- 3 egg yolks
- 175ml double cream
- 4 gelatine leaves
- Juice of a lemon
- 4 egg whites
- 8 tbs water

The Green, Washington Old Village, Tyne & Wear NE38 7AB
Tel: 0191 415 1788, www.blacksmithstable.co.uk

BOUCHON BISTROT

4-6 Gilesgate, Hexham, Northumberland NE46 3NJ, Tel: 01434 609 943, www.bouchonbistrot.co.uk

COGNAC
JACQUET

BOUCHON BISTROT

Bouchon brings a little corner of rural France to Northumberland. French-owned and run, this is the classic country bistrot (hence the classic French spelling, with a 't') where you can close your eyes and the tastes, smells and sounds of France are yours.

Our style is traditional; our signature menus featuring classics such as escargots with garlic and parsley butter, oxtail terrine, poulet au citron, rump of lamp with flageolet beans and tomato Provencale. Our classic desserts include clafoutis aux cerises, tarte tatin, crème caramel, and chocolate, vanilla and espresso pots.

Our French onion soup represents the essence of France in a single bowl; a simple and traditional dish prepared, like all our food, expertly, confidently and with respect for every ingredient.

Our dishes, like our restaurant, are fresh and uncomplicated, created from the finest produce, served simply and in season in the traditional French country way.

Long, laid-back lunches, big family dinners or romantic dining a deux: our 18th Century home in the heart of Hexham's historic leather tanning and merchants' quarter is warm and intimate; a little corner of France in the Tyne Valley.

Gregory Bureau, owner

4-6 Gilesgate, Hexham, Northumberland NE46 3NJ,
Tel: 01434 609 943, www.bouchonbistrot.co.uk

TUNA NIÇOISE

METHOD

For the sun blushed tomatoes: Half two tomatoes from top to bottom and cut each half into three. Place on a baking sheet with a sprig of Thyme and Rosemary and drizzle with olive oil. Sprinkle with the garlic and season well. Bake in a very slow oven (80-100°C) about 5 hrs. Allow to cool to room temperature.

For the soft boiled egg: Put the eggs into a pan of boiling water for 6½ mins. Put immediately into iced water. Peel when cooled then half and cut each half into three.

For the green beans: Put into a large pot of well salted, boiling water. Remove when they are no longer crunchy but still have some bite and put into iced water.

For the vinaigrette maison: Whisk the mustard, shallot, garlic and seasoning into the vinegar. Slowly add the oil while whisking vigorously to form an emulsion. (Tip: Put any left over dressing into a jam jar and if the dressing splits a good shake will bring it back together!)

To serve: Put a non stick pan onto a hot flame. Don't put any oil in yet. Prepare the salad by mixing the leaves, beans, red onion and olives with the dressing. Put a handful into the centre of a shallow bowl. Very lightly oil the pan and put your seasoned tuna steak straight on. Keep the heat on high. Put the tomatoes and egg around the edge of your salad and top with the anchovies. Turn the tuna over and cook for one more minute on the second side. Do not cook the tuna right through to the middle otherwise it will be extremely dry. Put the tuna onto the salad and serve immediately.

INGREDIENTS

Serves 4

SALAD:

- 4 x 100g portions of tuna loin
- 2 ripe plum tomatoes
- 1 clove of garlic (roughly chopped)
- 200g green beans
- 2 eggs
- 12 achovy fillets
- 4 handfuls of salad Leaves
- ½ diced red onion
- 1 handful of olives (Stoned and halved)
- Sprig of thyme & rosemary
- Salt & pepper
- Olive oil

BOUCHON VINAIGRETTE MAISON:

- 100ml red wine vinegar
- ½ teaspoon dijon mustard
- 1 banana shallot finely chopped
- 1 garlic clove finely chopped
- 200ml good quality olive oil

4-6 Gilesgate, Hexham, Northumberland NE46 3NJ,
Tel: 01434 609 943, www.bouchonbistrot.co.uk

CRISPY DUCK CONFIT WITH LYONNAISE POTATOES & BRAISED SAVOY CABBAGE

BOUCHON BISTROT

INGREDIENTS

Serves 4

DUCK:

- 4 plump duck legs
- Duck fat (enough to cover the legs in a deep tray)
- 100g rock sea salt
- 1 sprig of rosemary
- 1 sprig of thyme

GARNISH:

- 200g of Ratte potatoes
- 1 small savoy cabbage
- 1 small onion
- 100g of streaky bacon

SAUCE:

- 40cl of veal stock
- 1 dash of vider vinegar
- 1 sprig of rosemary
- 10g of butter

METHOD

For the Duck: Rub the salt with the herbs on the duck legs. Place the lot into a container with a lid. Leave in the fridge over night (12 hours maximum). Discard the salt and herbs, and soak the duck leg in cold water for 6 hours, changing the water every 1½ hours. Place the duck legs in a cast iron or oven proof casserole dish and cover them with duck fat. Put the casserole lid in place and cook in the oven at100˚C for 8 hours. Leave it to cool in the fat, and place it in the fridge. You can keep the legs for a couple of weeks, as long as they are covered in duck fat.

For the garnish: Cook the cabbage in salted boiled water for 3 minutes, refresh in ice cold water, and keep for serving later. Cut the streaky bacon into lardons.

For the sauce: Get the liquor from the duck legs – it should have set at the bottom of your casserole dish (it should be easy to separate the liquor, which will have a jelly consistency. Bring the liquor to the boil, add 5cl of cider vinegar, then 40cl of veal stock. Reduce to 2/3 . Keep for serving.

And finally: Place the duck legs in a hot oven 180°c for 10 minutes, pan fry the potatoes on a slow heat until light brown, then add the sliced onions, stir and cook until golden brown, stir on a regular basis. In a pan, sautéed the bacon on a medium heat, then add the cabbage. Cook for 5 minutes. Reheat the sauce slowly, when it has reached the boil, add a knob of butter and stir with a whisk (emulsify). Plate the Lyonnaise potatoes, then cabbage and the duck onto a plate. Pour the sauce over the meat and garnish. Bon Appétit!

4-6 Gilesgate, Hexham, Northumberland NE46 3NJ,
Tel: 01434 609 943, www.bouchonbistrot.co.uk

BOUCHON BISTROT

APPLE TARTE TATIN

METHOD

To prepare: Pre heat your oven @165c make a caramel by putting the caster sugar into a heavy duty frying pan, until the sugar starts melting, stir with a wooden spoon until it turns into a liquid. Continue to stir until you get a deep golden colour. Then place the butter in the frying pan and stir vigorously, until the caramel settles. As soon as the caramel is golden brown, remove from the heat, then stir until it cools down to a toffee consistency.

For the tart: Peel the apples and then slice in half from top to bottom. Arrange in a deep sauté frying pan, starting at the outer edge and working around in a circular motion. Pack the apples in tight enough to support one another, making sure the apples will be fitted tightly as they shrink during cooking. Bake the apples uncovered in the oven for 45 minutes untill softened. Remove and allow to cool to room temperature. Turn your oven to 180°C. Roll out the puff pastry and cut a disk one centimeter larger than the frying pan. Place on top of the apples and fold the lip under around the circumference. Prick the puff pastry to allow steam to escape, which will give you a crisp base. Bake for a further 25 minutes until the pastry is golden brown. Remove from the oven and allow to cool for 10 minutes. Run a pallet knike around the outside of the tart, then place a chopping board on top of the pan. In one motion, flip the pan upside down allowing the tart to release from the pan. Serve at once with a generous scoop of vanilla ice cream. Voilà!

INGREDIENTS

Serves 4

- 180g caster sugar
- 120g unsalted butter (cut into cubes)
- 8 medium sized golden delicious apples
- 300g puff pastry

4-6 Gilesgate, Hexham, Northumberland NE46 3NJ,
Tel: 01434 609 943, www.bouchonbistrot.co.uk

CHATEAU

CAFÉ LOWREY

33-35 The Broadway, Darras Hall, Ponteland, Newcastle Upon Tyne NE20 9PW, Tel: 01661 820 357, www.cafelowrey.co.uk

White Wine by the Glass
Piper Heidsieck Champagne
Side Dishes
Crispy Onions
Mixed Vegetables
Buttered Spinach
Hand Cut Chips
New Potatoes
£2.50

cafe Low
IAN LOW

At Café Lowrey our food is deliberately uncomplicated and our aim is to make the best use of the finest, fresh local produce. I took over the restaurant four years ago, having been head chef there for some years when it was known as Café 21.

It is a labour of love, I know the place well and am continuing the ethos of quality food, which I have experienced as a chef working in well-known restaurants all over the region. I know and appreciate the importance of creating a warm, relaxed and inviting environment where diners can really enjoy their food and know that it is the best it can be. We strive at Café Lowrey to ensure that this is always the case.

Ian Lowrey, owner

33-35 The Broadway, Darras Hall, Ponteland, Newcastle Upon Tyne NE20 9PW
Tel: 01661 820 357, www.cafelowrey.co.uk

CRAB & PICKLED GINGER RISOTTO

METHOD

To prepare: Heat a pan and gently fry the shallots in some of the butter for 3-4 minutes until soft but without colouring.

For the risotto: Add the rice and cover with the fish stock. Simmer gently and stir constantly until all of the liquid has been absorbed - the rice should be slightly 'al dente.'

To finish: Add the crab, ginger, chives, spring onions, Parmesan and 2 knobs of butter to the rice, stirring until it thickens, then serve.

INGREDIENTS

Serves 2

- 150g Arborio rice
- 1 shallot (finely chopped)
- 200 ml fish stock
- 1 bunch chives (chopped)
- 100g butter
- 100g white crab meat
- 50g pickled ginger (chopped)
- 50g parmesan (grated)
- 2 spring onions (chopped)

33-35 The Broadway, Darras Hall, Ponteland, Newcastle Upon Tyne NE20 9PW
Tel: 01661 820 357, www.cafelowrey.co.uk

Lowrey

MOROCCAN CHICKEN, COUSCOUS & MINT, LEMON & YOGHURT DRESSING

INGREDIENTS

Serves 4

4 chicken breasts
200g couscous
100ml chicken stock

DRESSING:

200ml natural yoghurt
Juice from 1 lemon
5 mint leaves (finely chopped)

MARINADE:

200ml natural yoghurt
100g Moroccan spices
1 red chilli
10 sprigs coriander (chopped)
2 cloves of garlic (chopped)

METHOD

To prepare: Combine all of the ingredients for the marinade, place the chicken breasts in the marinade and leave overnight in the fridge.

For the chicken: Take the chicken breasts out of the marinade, pan fry to colour then bake in the oven for15-20 minutes until cooked at 180˚C.

For the couscous: Bring the chicken stock to the boil, stir in the couscous, cover with cling-film and leave for 5 minutes.

For the dressing: Combine the yoghurt, lemon juice and chopped mint together and mix well.

To serve: Place the couscous in the centre of the plate, cut the chicken breast into three pieces and place on top of the couscous. Pour the dressing over and serve.

33-35 The Broadway, Darras Hall, Ponteland, Newcastle Upon Tyne NE20 9PW
Tel: 01661 820 357, www.cafelowrey.co.uk

CHOCOLATE TART

METHOD

For the pastry: Rub the butter into the flour and sugar and mix until it has a texture of coarse breadcrumbs, then add the egg mixture (1 egg and 1 egg yolk) and bring together into a dough. Wrap in cling film and leave to rest for 30 minutes in the fridge.

For the chocolate filling: Place the cream into a pan and bring to just under the boil. Whisk together the egg yolks and sugar, then add the cream to the egg mixture. Stir in the chocolate and allow to melt. Skim the foam off the top of the mixture and pass through a sieve.

For the chestnut cream: Whip the cream and sugar into stiff peaks. Add the chestnut puree to taste.

To finish: Roll out the pastry and line a 12 inch tart case and bake blind at 150˚C for approx 30-35 minutes. Pour in the chocolate mixture and bake at 110˚C for a further approx 30-40 minutes or until just set. Serve with the chestnut cream.

INGREDIENTS

Serves 12

PASTRY:
- 250g plain flour
- 150g unsalted butter
- 25g sugar
- 1 egg
- 1 egg yolk

CHOCOLATE FILLING :
- 800m1 plain flour
- 200g egg yolks (approx10 eggs)
- 125g sugar
- 175g dark chocolate

CHESTNUT CREAM :
- 400ml double cream
- 2 tbs icing sugar
- 100g chestnut puree

33-35 The Broadway, Darras Hall, Ponteland, Newcastle Upon Tyne NE20 9PW
Tel: 01661 820 357, www.cafelowrey.co.uk

Lowrey

CASEY'S BRASSERIE

113a High Street, Great Ayton, North Yorkshire TS9 6BW, Tel: 01642 724204

I have had a really interesting food journey, working with some top establishments and some fine chefs, which has enabled me to combine the skills and experiences gained along the way and incorporate them into my own restaurant. The result is Casey's Brasserie, offering simple and wholesome British food, using seasonal ingredients at an affordable price.

I opened my light and airy restaurant in the pretty village of Great Ayton wanting it to be the perfect antidote to the rush and hustle of modern life. Nestling in the Cleveland Hills, it is the perfect stopping off point after a leisurely day out exploring this lovely area of North Yorkshire, midway between the coast and the Dales.

Already popular with locals, it's a secret gem which is fast gaining a reputation for fabulous food with a fresh and contemporary style. My cooking is British with Mediterranean influences and the menu is updated with produce as it comes into season. We offer mouth-watering real food with a good balance of flavours.

The kitchen brigade, which includes my son Danny, prepares the freshest local ingredients and reflects the local bounty of fish from Whitby, meat sourced from the region's farmers and tip-top vegetables and dairy produce. Cooking has always been in my blood and I've honed my talents in a wide variety of establishments - including a brief, but invaluable stint with Gary Rhodes - before opening my own restaurant. My passion is to offer people a great dining experience.

Jennifer Veale, owner

113a High Street, Great Ayton, North Yorkshire TS9 6BW
Tel: 01642 724204

PAN FRIED HALIBUT WITH SMOOTH ROAST TOMATO SAUCE, BUTTERBEANS, CHORIZO AND BLACK PUDDING

METHOD

For the tomato sauce: Quarter the tomatoes and place on a baking tray. Sprinkle lightly with salt, pepper and caster sugar. Roast at 200°C for 20 minutes or until soft. Sweat the onion in the oil for 5 minutes, add the garlic and celery and coat in oil. Lightly crush the fennel seed in a pestle and mortar and add to the pan. Add the roasted tomatoes and stir all the ingredients. Add the stock or water and bring to the boil, reduce the heat to simmer and cook until the liquid has reduced by one third (this should take about half an hour). Cool, and blitz the sauce in a food processor and then push through a sieve. Adjust with more liquid to get the consistency you require. Taste and adjust the seasoning. If the sauce is too sharp add a splash of lemon juice and caster sugar to taste.

For the garnish: Brown the chorizo all over and cook as ordinary sausage (approx 10 minutes over a low heat). Cool and slice diagonally. Dice the black pudding and pan fry for 5 minutes (keep warm). Rinse the butterbeans and heat. Reheat the tomato sauce.

For the fish: In a hot frying pan add 1 Tbs of olive and heat. Pan fry the seasoned halibut skin side down for 3 minutes. Turn the fish over and continue to cook for a further 2 to 3 minutes (depending on thickness). **To serve:** Spoon some of the warm butterbeans into the centre of the plate, pour around the tomato sauce, and place the halibut on top of the butterbeans. Garnish with the chorizo, black pudding and remaining butterbeans. I use Taste of Tradition (Thirsk) pork chorizo and Petch (Great Ayton) black pudding.

INGREDIENTS

Serves 4

- 4 x halibut fillets (approx 200g each)
- Chorizo sausages (raw)200g
- 2 tins of butterbeans
- 250g black pudding
- 1 tsp olive oil

TOMATO SAUCE:

- 8 large vine tomatoes
- 1 large onion (diced)
- 2 garlic cloves (roughly chopped)
- 1 celery stick (sliced)
- 2 tsp fennel seeds
- 1 tsp (approx) olive oil
- 1 litre veg stock / or water
- Salt and pepper
- Caster sugar

113a High Street, Great Ayton, North Yorkshire TS9 6BW
Tel: 01642 724204

RESERVE WENSLEYDALE SAUSAGES, WITH RED ONION, CIDER AND APPLE SALAD AND ROAST BEETROOT

INGREDIENTS

Serves 4

SAUSAGES:
- 175 g fresh breadcrumbs
- 175g reserve Wensleydale cheese
- 2 tbs chopped chives
- 1 whole egg (large free range)
- 1 egg yolk (large free range)
- 1 tsp dry mustard powder
- Salt and pepper
- Approx 100ml milk to bind
- Oil to fry

ONIONS:
- 2 red onions (peeled and sliced)
- 1 tbs olive oil
- 4 tbs demerara sugar
- 1 tsp wholegrain mustard
- 500ml dry cider

BEETROOT GARNISH:
- 2 beetroot
- 2 red dessert apples
- Chives chopped

METHOD

For the onions: Heat the oil and sweat the sliced onions over a medium heat for 15 minutes, stirring occasionally. Add the sugar just as the onions begin to brown and stir to dissolve. Add the cider and grain mustard. Reduce over a low heat until the liquid has evaporated. Set aside, serve cold or reheat in a pan.

For the sausages: Mix together all of the dry ingredients and cheese. Beat the egg and yolk together and incorporate the dry ingredients with a wooden spoon. Add the milk bit by bit to achieve the correct consistency. The mixture should stick easily when you roll it in a ball. Divide the mixture into 12 and shape into small sausages (refrigerate until needed). Pan fry the sausages over a medium heat in hot oil for approx 10 minutes

For the beetroot: Wash the whole beetroot thoroughly. Cook in the oven at 200°C for approx 1 hour or until tender (like a baked potato). Cool, peel and cut into wedges.

To serve: Place the hot sausages on top of the onions. Garnish with beetroot wedges, apple slices and chives and a drizzle of grain mustard dressing.

113a High Street, Great Ayton, North Yorkshire TS9 6BW
Tel: 01642 724204

CHOCOLATE AND RASPBERRY CREAM ROULADE, RASPBERRY JELLY AND SAUCE

INGREDIENTS

Serves 8

ROULADE:
- 6 large free range eggs (separated)
- 150g caster sugar
- 60g cocoa powder (plus extra for dusting)
- Splash of raspberry liqueur or rum

ROULADE FILLING:
- 300ml double cream
- 100g icing sugar (vary for personal taste)
- Half a vanilla pod
- 500g fresh raspberries

JELLY:
- 200g fresh raspberries
- 500 ml water
- 250g caster sugar
- 3 leaves of gelatine

SAUCE:
- 300g fresh raspberries
- 2 tbs icing sugar
- 2 tbs water
- Splash of lemon juice

CHOCOLATE SHAPES:
- 250g Dark chocolate (70 cocoa solids)

METHOD

For the roulade: Heat the oven to 190˚C. Grease and line a 22 x 32 cm Swiss roll tin with silicone paper. Whisk the egg yolks and sugar until doubled in volume and fluffy. Sift the cocoa into the yolk mixture and fold. Whisk the egg whites in a clean, grease free bowl until stiff (but not too dry). Fold the whites into the chocolate mix one third at a time using a metal spoon. Pour the mixture onto the lined tin and smooth it to the edges. Bake for approx 15 minutes until firm and light. Let it cool in the tin. Dust a similar sized sheet of silicone paper with cocoa, and turn out the sponge face down onto it. It helps to have a clean damp tea towel underneath the dusted silicone sheet. Whip the cream and icing sugar until soft peas, scrape out the vanilla seeds and add to the mixture. Sprinkle the liqueur / rum over the roulade base. Add the cream and smooth to cover. Arrange the raspberries evenly on top of the cream (avoid the edges by 2 cm as it will spread when rolling). Roll the roulade away from you swiftly. Cling film the roulade in the paper for at least one hour before slicing.

For the jelly: Simmer the water and sugar until the sugar has dissolved. Soak the gelatine leaves in cold water until soft. Squeeze with your hands and add to the stock syrup. Whisk until the gelatine dissolves and remove from the heat. Add the raspberries. When a little cooler, blend into a liquid. Pass through a fine sieve and pour into shot glasses. When cool refrigerate for approx 2 - 3 hours to set.

For the sauce: Blitz all the ingredients together and pass through a fine sieve.

To serve: Slice the roulade and decorate with the sauce, jelly and chocolate shapes

113a High Street, Great Ayton, North Yorkshire TS9 6BW
Tel: 01642 724204

CHAR MAUSAM

Station Road End, Stannington, Morpeth, Northumberland NE61 6DR, Tel: 01670 789011

The successful formula popularised in the 1980's north Indian menus, the Raj-inspired decor and the papadoms and lager combination – was by the 1990's beginning to look jaded. Having won Britain's hearts the curry house experience was beginning to lose its charm through over familiarity. From the outset it was our aim to address these issues

However, the choice of location for our restaurant did initially raised a lot of eyebrows, A run down Little Chef by the by-passed A1 didn't seem a great location for an Indian restaurant, a lot of people did question our judgement (or madness), However, in the three years we have been here, we have managed to establish the restaurant as one of the best in the region.

Our menu draws inspiration from various regions of India, (whose own culinary history has been influenced by its many foreign rulers), offering a variety of regional dishes which show off the wonderful cooking styles of India, with a special emphasis on fish and game.

Mohammed Iqbal, Rafiquzzaman Choudhury, Jehadul Haque, owners

Station Road End, Stannington, Morpeth,
Northumberland NE61 6DR Tel: 01670 789011

CHOLE AUR CAJU CHAT

METHOD

Heat some oil in a frying pan and fry the garlic paste until it starts to brown, add the onions, mix in the chillis, tomato puree, methi leaves, curry powder, cumin powder,chat masala and stir, add the potatoes, chickpeas, cashew nuts and sultanas and stir until well combined. Serve on a bed of salad leaves either warm or cold and garnish with coriander.

INGREDIENTS

Serves 4

300g boiled chickpeas
250g cashew nuts
100g sultanas
1 large potato
(boiled and cut into small dice)
1 small onion (chopped)
2 green chilli
(deseeded and chopped, leave the seeds if you want it spicy)
1 tbs chopped fresh coriander
1 tsp tomato puree
1 tsp methi leaves
1 tbs garlic paste
1 tsp chat masala
1 tsp curry powder
1 tsp cumin powder
1 tbs vegetable oil

Station Road End, Stannington, Morpeth,
Northumberland NE61 6DR Tel: 01670 789011

GOAN FISH CURRY

INGREDIENTS

Serves 4

- 800g salmon fillets
- 6-8 cloves of garlic, (finely chopped)
- 2cm piece of fresh root ginger (finely shredded)
- 2 medium onions (finely chopped)
- 2 green chillies (deseeded if you want the flavour rather than the heat)
- 2 tsp ground cumin
- 2 tsp ground coriander
- 2 tsp curry powder
- 2 tsp ground turmeric
- 200ml water or fish stock
- 1 tbs tamarind concentrated
- 200ml coconut milk
- 1 tbs tomato puree
- 5 tbs vegetable oil
- 2 tbs chopped coriander
- Salt to taste

METHOD

For the fish: Marinate the fish with 1 tsp turmeric and 1 tbs vegetable oil, heat a non-stick pan and sear the fish for about 5 minutes or until golden brown (this gives the fish a crunchy coating while keeping the centre moist) and set aside.

For the curry: Heat oil in a large pan and fry the garlic until it starts to brown, add the onions, ginger, green chilli and the tomato puree. Sauté until it softens, add all the powder, spices and cook, stirring frequently, until the oil begins to separate out from it. Add the water (fish stock), coconut milk and bring to the boil. Stir in the tamarind pulp and simmer for 5 minutes, check the consistency. It should be like a pouring sauce, if it is too thin simmer for a little longer, taste and adjust the seasoning if necessary. Now add the fish and simmer over a medium heat for 3-4 minutes without stirring. Remove from the heat, cover the pan and stand for 5 minutes to allow the fish to cook in the heat from the sauce. Serve with some basmati rice. And garnish with some chopped coriander.

Station Road End, Stannington, Morpeth,
Northumberland NE61 6DR Tel: 01670 789011

GAJAR KA HALWA

METHOD

Put the grated carrots, milk and cardamom pods in a heavy-bottomed saucepan and bring to the boil. Turn heat to medium and cook, stirring now and then until all the liquid has evaporated, about 1 hour to 1 1/2 hours, adjust the heat if you need to. Melt the butter or ghee in a non-stick frying pan over a medium-low heat, and add to the carrot mixture, stir and fry until the carrots no longer have a wet, milky look. They should turn a rich, reddish colour. This may take 15-20 minutes. Add the sugar, sultanas and pistachios and stir and fry for another 2 minutes. To serve, spoon the halwa into a lightly greased 6-7cm cutter on individual plates. Smooth the surface to shape neatly, and carefully lift off the cutter. Top each serving with a scoop of ginger ice cream (you can use other flavours, preferably ones that are sharp tasting), and mint sprig. Scatter some crushed pistachio around the halwa.

INGREDIENTS

Serves 4

1kg carrots (peeled and finely grated)
1 litre full fat milk
8 whole cardamom pods
100g ghee or unsalted butter
200g sugar
100g unsalted pistachios, (lightly crushed)
100g raisins or sultanas

Station Road End, Stannington NE61 6DR
Tel: 01670 789011/789012

THE CHERRY TREE

9 Osborne Road, Jesmond, Newcastle upon Tyne, NE2 2AE, Tel: 0191 239 9924, www.thecherrytreejesmond.co.uk

The food philosophy of The Cherry Tree is to use quality local ingredients in simple, uncomplicated dishes. Our menu has been cleverly planned to make the most of seasonal produce with dishes to suit everyone's tastes. We aim to provide the best modern British & European cuisine in the North East with timeless classics as well as dishes with a more contemporary twist. Begin with North Shield's crab with soft shell crab tempura or soothing leek & potato soup with native oyster & caviar cream. Move onto mains of rump of Ingram Valley lamb or local caught turbot with king prawns, Yukon Gold mash & lobster bisque sauce, before giving in to sticky toffee & pecan pavlova or white chocolate & macadamia nut parfait. We also offer a small selection of some of the best artisan cheeses produced in Britain today. An eclectic list of sixty eight wines cover most wine producing regions of the world.

In a short time, the Cherry Tree has earned itself a reputation for being a great place to enjoy modern British food. The restaurant gives customers a stunning dining experience, featuring a mezzanine floor with glass balustrade and open spiral staircase, a double height ceiling shows off beautiful focal point lighting and big, globular lights made of twisted silver, but retaining some of the older features of the building, previously the Jesmond telephone exchange and the Scout shop.

Service is friendly, creating a relaxed atmosphere with live background music played most evening.

Tony Riches, head chef

9 Osborne Road, Jesmond, Newcastle upon Tyne, NE2 2AE
Tel: 0191 239 9924, www.thecherrytreejesmond.co.uk

WARM HAM HOCK SALAD WITH SOFT BOILED FREE RANGE EGG, GARDEN PEAS & MUSTARD

METHOD

For the ham: Place the rinsed ham shank into a pan deep enough to comfortably hold it. Add enough water to cover the ham. Bring to the boil and reduce the heat to a simmer. Skim off any fat or scum which rises to the surface. Add the vegetables, bay leaves, peppercorns and vinegar and cook for approx 3 hrs or until the smaller of the two bones pull out easily. Allow to cool slightly then pulls away the covering fat and break the meat into little finger sized pieces.

For the eggs: Cook the eggs in boiling water for 4 ½ mins and immediately refresh in cold water. Peel and set aside.

For the peas: Shell the peas and place into salted boiling water and cook for 2 mins. Drain, refresh and set aside.

To make the dressing: Place the mustard into a stainless steel whisking bowl with the vinegar and a touch of salt and pepper. Whisking all the time, gradually drizzle in the olive oil until well emulsified. Check the seasoning.

To serve: Cut each egg in half and place the two halfs in the middle of a plate. Dress the peas with a little of the dressing. Arrange an equal amount on each plate scattering the peas randomly. Place the warm ham amongst the peas. Snip the pea shoots from the punnet and place 4 or 5 shoots onto each plate. Season the egg yolk with a pinch of sea salt & a twist of white pepper.

INGREDIENTS

Serves 4

- 1 ham hock or shank (soaked in cold water for 24 hours)
- 2 carrots (peeled and roughly chopped)
- 2 onions (peeled & roughly chopped)
- 2 sticks of celery (roughly chopped)
- 1 tsp whole white peppercorns
- 2 bay leaves
- 50ml white wine vinegar
- 4 eggs
- 1lb peas
- 1 punnet of pea shoots
- 100ml extra virgin olive oil
- 20ml white wine vinegar
- 1tsp coarse wholegrain mustard

9 Osborne Road, Jesmond, Newcastle upon Tyne, NE2 2AE
Tel: 0191 239 9924, www.thecherrytreejesmond.co.uk

WILD SEA BASS WITH ARTICHOKES & COURGETTES

INGREDIENTS

Serves 4

- 4 x50oz sea bass fillets (boned & scaled)
- 4 Petit Violet or small artichokes (trimmed)
- 1 lemon
- 4 Charlotte potatoes or similar large new potato
- 16 cherry plum tomatoes (or cherry vine tomatoes)
- 2 medium courgettes
- Olive oil
- Salt & pepper

SALSA VERDE :

- 1 bunch flat parsley
- 1 bunch basil
- 1 bunch mint
- 2 cloves of garlic
- 1 tbs Dijon mustard
- 2 tbs white wine vinegar
- 1 heaped tbs capers (not salted ones)
- 100ml olive oil

METHOD

For the artichokes: Holding the artichoke by the stem, pull away the coarse and tough outside leaves until the paler leaves are visible. Using a sharp knife trim away the thick 'skin' that covers the base and stem. Drop into a bowl of cold water with the juice of the lemon squeezed in. Pour the contents of the bowl into a stainless steel pan, season with salt & cook for approx 10 minutes or until the tip of a small sharp knife pierces the artichoke with a little resistance. Remove from the heat and leave to cool in the liquor.

For the potatoes: Boil the potatoes in salted water until cooked, remove from the water and allow to cool.

For the courgetts: Using a mandolin or bread knife cut the courgettes into strips. Brush each strip with olive oil and cook on a char grill pan. Remove and cool.

For the salsa: Place all ingredients except the oil into a food processor and blend. With the motor still running, gradually pour in the olive oil to emulsify the sauce. Season with salt & pepper.

For the fish: Score the skin of each sea bass fillet and season with sea salt & white pepper. Add a splash of olive oil to a non stick frying pan and when hot, place the sea bass fillet skin side down. Season the flesh side of the fish and allow to cook 2-3 minutes before turning over and cooking on the other side for another 2-3 minutes. When cooked, season with a squeeze of lemon and set aside on a warmed plate. Wipe out the pan with absorbent paper and add another splash of olive oil. Cut the potatoes into 1/4 quaters length ways. Fry for a minute. Add the artichoke halves. Add a knob of butter and when the potatoes & artichokes are golden brown, add the cherry tomatoes and courgettes. When the tomatoes have softened a little remove from the heat and arrange in the centre of 4 warmed serving plates. Place the fish on top and pour around some salsa verde.

9 Osborne Road, Jesmond, Newcastle upon Tyne, NE2 2AE
Tel: 0191 239 9924, www.thecherrytreejesmond.co.uk

NEW SEASONS RHUBARB & CUSTARD TRIFLE

METHOD

To make the sponge: Mix together the butter & sugar until light & creamy. Add the vanilla essence and eggs, one at time until fully incorporated. Sift the flour into the butter mix and gently fold in. Pour into a lined 8" cake tin and bake at 180˚c for 20-25 mins. Allow to cool on a wire rack before turning out.

For the jelly: Soak the gelatine in cold water for 10 minutes until soft and pliable. Bring the sugar and water to the boil, and then add the rhubarb and grenadine. Lower the heat and poach gently for 5 minutes until the rhubarb is soft but not breaking up. Remove the rhubarb from the stock syrup and set aside. Squeeze any excess water from the gelatine and mix into the hot syrup along with the champagne or prosecco. Allow to cool to room temperature. To assemble the first stage, dice up the sponge to 1/2 square cubes and place in a glass with some of the rhubarb, to come 1/3 up the glass. Pour over the liquid jelly mix and allow to soak for 5 minutes. Place in the fridge to set up.

For the custard: Place the double cream, 1/2 the sugar and vanilla into a pan and bring to the boil mixing all the time. Remove from the heat and allow to infuse for 5 minutes. Place the egg yolks and remaining sugar into a stainless steel bowl and whisk until the eggs become lighter in colour and texture. Pour the cream mix through a sieve onto the egg yolk mix whisking all the time. Return the pan to a low heat and stir with a wooden spoon for 5 minutes or until a food probe shows a temperature of 84˚C. Pour into a bowl set over another larger bowl containing ice & water. When cooled and starting to thicken, pour over the set jelly, leaving the top third of the glass empty. Place back in the fridge.

To serve: spoon some whipped cream on top of the trifle and sprinkle over the praline and serve straight away.

INGREDIENTS

Serves 4

JELLY:
- 500g rhubarb (cut into half inch pieces)
- 100g castor sugar
- 200ml water
- 4 sheets gelatine
- 200ml champagne or prosecco
- 50ml grenadine

SPONGE:
- 175 g self raising flour
- 1tsp baking powder
- 175g softened butter
- 175g castor sugar
- 3 eggs
- 1/2 tsp vanilla essence

CUSTARD:
- 7 egg yolks
- 100g caster sugar
- 500ml double cream
- 1 vanilla pod

TO SERVE:
- Whipped cream

9 Osborne Road, Jesmond, Newcastle upon Tyne, NE2 2AE
Tel: 0191 239 9924, www.thecherrytreejesmond.co.uk

CLOSE HOUSE HOTEL

Located in the Northumberland countryside within the magnificent setting of Close House, Bewickes Restaurant is the perfect meeting place for business lunches, ladies' lunches, dinner with family and friends or to celebrate a special occasion. Close House is open to all and is a perfect location with its proximity to Newcastle, only 15 minutes away from the city centre, and about the same distance from Hexham.

Our main aim is to pursue and purvey the freshest and, most importantly, seasonal produce from around the region and treat this produce with the respect it deserves. We source some of the finest quality ingredients from specialist suppliers from the region as well as from across the UK and Europe. We offer a great selection of contemporary cuisine with a French influence.

Bewickes Restaurant will give you one of the finest dining experiences available in the North East. The décor is sumptuous and modern with a classical theme and we strive to give a sense of genuine welcome, comfort and relaxation.

Chris Delaney, head chef

Bewickes Restaurant, Heddon on the Wall, Newcastle Upon Tyne, NE15 0HT
Tel: 01661 852 255, www.closehouse.co.uk

OXTAIL PLATE

METHOD

For the oxtail terrine: Remove the oxtails from cooking liquor, pass the liquor through a fine sieve and reduce by half. Pick the meat from oxtails and keep warm. Soften the vegetables, add the oxtail meat and reduced cooking liquor. Cook until thick and press into a terrine lined with cling film. Chill for 24 hours.

For the oxtail and chilli consommé: Pass the beef and all of the vegetables through a mincer. Add the egg whites and season with soy sauce, salt and pepper. In a pan, gradually add the stock to the mince, stirring all the time. Bring it up to heat until the mince forms a raft. Reduce heat to a very gentle simmer and cook for about an hour. Carefully pass through a muslin cloth and chill.

For the oxtail won tons: Soften the shallots, garlic, spring onions, ginger, lemon grass and chilli in a little oil. Scrape into a bowl and allow to cool a little. Add the cooked oxtail meat, soy sauce and milled pepper. Mix until a sticky mixture forms. Moisten the won ton wrappers with a little water, place a small ball of oxtail mix onto won ton, fold over and seal. Deep fry at 160°C.

To serve: Serve on a plate with a slice of terrine, a demitasse (cup) of consommé and a fried won ton and garnish with a port syrup and wasabi paste.

INGREDIENTS

Serves 4

OXTAIL TERRINE:

- 2kg slowly braised oxtails
- 1 each of carrot, onion, stick of celery (finely diced)
- 2 fat garlic cloves (finely diced)
- 200ml red wine
- Salt and pepper

OXTAIL AND CHILLI CONSOMMÉ:

- 2 litres good oxtail stock (chilled)
- 500g shin of beef
- 1 each of carrot, onion, stick of celery, leek (white part only)
- 4 hot chilli peppers
- Few thyme sprigs
- 4 egg whites
- Soy sauce

OXTAIL WON TONS:

- 4 won ton wrappers
- 75g picked oxtail meat (cooked)
- 1 shallot (finely diced)
- 2 spring onions (finely sliced)
- 1 garlic clove (crushed)
- 1 green chilli finely chopped
- 1 thumb size piece ginger (finely grated)
- 1 lemon grass stalk (inner stem only, finely chopped)
- Splash of Kikkoman soy sauce

Bewickes Restaurant, Heddon on the Wall, Newcastle Upon Tyne, NE15 0HT
Tel: 01661 852 255, www.closehouse.co.uk

HERB ROASTED SPRING CHICKEN BALLOTINE WITH FOIE GRAS AND TRUFFLE CHICKEN AND TARRAGON ESSENCE

INGREDIENTS

Serves 4

- 4 spring chickens or poussin
- 2 litres good chicken stock
- 40g foie gras (diced)
- 2 tsp diced truffle or truffle peelings (finely chopped)
- 500ml white wine
- 4 Heritage potatoes (cooked and peeled)
- 16 asparagus tips (blanched)
- 16 sml morel mushrooms
- 16 sml St. George Mousseron mushrooms
- 100g chicken mousse
- 50g tarragon
- 100g herb butter (soft)
- 250ml cream
- Butter
- Salt and pepper
- Parsley (chopped)

METHOD

For the chicken: Using fingers, prize skin away from flesh on the breasts. With a piping bag, force the butter up and over the breasts, under the skin and smooth over using cling film. Chill. Remove the legs and carefully bone out using a sharp knife. Place the boned out leg meat on a sheet of cling film overlapping each other (2 legs per sheet). Season with salt and pepper. Add half of the truffle and the diced foie gras to the chicken mousse along with a few of the tarragon leaves. Divide the mousse between the legs and roll in cling film into a tight sausage and chill.

For the sauce: Reduce the chicken stock, wine and tarragon together until just syrupy. Add cream, bring to the boil and cook until it starts to thicken. Remove from heat and keep warm. Just before serving, blitz 75g butter into the sauce over heat.

To assemble: Season the chicken crowns with salt and white pepper. Place in oven 170°C. Cook for 14 minutes. Remove from oven and rest in a warm place for 10 minutes. At the same time, steam the chicken ballotines for 18-20 minutes. Allow to rest. Cook the morels and St George's mushrooms in a little butter. Warm the potatoes and season with sea salt, butter, chopped truffle and chopped parsley. Heat the asparagus tips and season with salt. Remove ballotines from cling film, slice off both ends then cut in half. Remove the breasts from the crown and arrange on warm plates, finishing with the sauce.

Bewickes Restaurant, Heddon on the Wall, Newcastle Upon Tyne, NE15 0HT
Tel: 01661 852 255, www.closehouse.co.uk

CLOSE HOUSE HOTEL

RASPBERRY AND WHITE CHOCOLATE 'TRIFLE' AND BASIL PANACOTTA

METHOD

For the panacotta: Boil the cream, sugar, vanilla and basil. Add the gelatine then pass through a sieve and allow to cool. When beginning to set, add the Bacardi and pour into shallow tray. Freeze then cut out small rounds.

For the raspberry jelly: Warm the puree and dissolve gelatine into it. Allow to set then cut into cubes.

For the raspberry coulis: Mix the frozen raspberries and sugar together and leave to defrost. Blitz in a food processor then pass through a sieve to remove seeds.

For the vanilla sponge: Cream the butter, vanilla paste and sugar together until light and fluffy. Slowly add the eggs, beating well, then fold in the flour. Spread onto a baking tray and cook at 175˚C for approximately 6–10 minutes. Once cooled, sandwich together with raspberry jam and brush with framboise syrup.

For the white chocolate bavarois: Boil the milk with half of the sugar. Whisk the yolks with the other half of the sugar. When boiling, temper onto yolks, to avoid scrambling, then return mixture to the pan and cook until 85°C stirring all the time. Add soaked gelatine and pass onto chocolate. Allow to cool then fold in semi whipped cream. Pipe into forms, lined with discs of framboise syrup soaked sponge. Smooth the top and leave to set. Serve with raspberries and deep fried basil.

INGREDIENTS

Serves 4

PANACOTTA:
- 1 litre double cream
- 2 vanilla pods (split and seeds scraped)
- 3 leaves gelatine (soaked in cold water)
- 160g sugar
- 25ml Bacardi
- 10g basil (finely chopped)

RASPBERRY JELLY:
- 500ml raspberry puree (reduced to thicken)
- 5 leaves gelatine (soaked in cold water)

RASPBERRY COULIS:
- 1kg frozen raspberries
- 335g caster sugar

VANILLA SPONGE:
- 120g castor sugar
- 120g unsalted butter
- 2 eggs
- 120g self-raising flour
- Vanilla paste

WHITE CHOCOLATE BAVAROIS:
- 450ml milk
- 145g castor sugar
- 4 egg yolks
- 30g gelatine (soaked in cold water)
- 360g white chocolate
- 450ml cream (semi whipped)

Bewickes Restaurant, Heddon on the Wall, Newcastle Upon Tyne, NE15 0HT
Tel: 01661 852 255, www.closehouse.co.uk

182 - 186 Ocean Road, South Shields NE33 2JQ, Tel: 0191 456 1202, www.colmansfishandchips.com

COLMAN'S OF SOUTH SHIELDS

Colman's
of South Shields
Fish & Chip Restaurant & Takeaway
(Est. 1926)
ACTS ABOUT OUR FISH & CHIPS
1. We use only wild fish (not farmed)
2. All our fish comes from sustainable fishing grounds
3. We use only fresh potatoes (Maris Piper or similar) which are prepared daily on the premises
4. We use only vegetable
from additives, low
in trans fat, contains
nated fats and no
nut produce
5. Our oil is contin
waste oil is
collected and is
6. We use a thick c
to provide a much
osorbency of oil
At Colma
a produ
oduce
hould you ha
lity.
our produc
ies about
ager.

Est 1926
FISH & CHIPS

Colmans of South Shields was established in 1926, and we have provided the people of the North East with the finest quality Fish and Chips and seafoods for four generations, and I firmly believe we are priviledged to be situated in the North East where we have access to some of the finest seafoods in the world. Over the last few years we have won several awards including best UK takeaway at the BBC Food and Farming Awards, we were also crowned Englands number one Fish and Chip shop at the Fish and Chip shop of the year awards. Recently we became national champion of Gary Rhodes' UKTV Local Food Heroes Award, we won this award by showcasing the quality of produce our region has to offer. The three dishes that we have featured are all dishes that we sell in the restaurant on a daily basis. They are simple, quick and easy to follow, just remember to use the finest ingredients available. At Colmans we only use fish that come from sustainable stocks, so please ask your fishmonger how your fish is sourced, it is really important!

Finally I hope you really enjoy trying these recipes, happy cooking.

Richard Ord

182 - 186 Ocean Road, South Shields NE33 2JQ
Tel: 0191 456 1202, www.colmansfishandchips.com

SALMON AND COD FISHCAKES

METHOD

For the fishcakes: Roughly cut the Salmon and Cod into approx 1"-2" squares, season with Salt and Pepper and steam until cooked, when cooked, chill immediately until cold (between 1°c - 4°c). Place fish into a bowl with Spring Onions, Herbs, Mayonnaise & Lemon Juice. Mix gently together until everything is bound together, (Take care not to mix too hard otherwise the Fish will turn to purée), taste the mix for seasoning, and add more if necessary. Shape the mix into four equal sized cakes. Place the Flour, Eggs and Breadcrumbs into 3 separate bowls, pass each cake, first through the flour, shaking off any excess, then through the egg and finally coat well in Breadcrumbs. Reshape the cakes, ensuring that they are coated well in Breadcrumbs. Heat the oil in a pan, add the Butter and cook Fishcakes until Golden Brown and crispy, make sure Fishcakes are hot in the middle, and if necessary, place into a heated oven at 160°c - 180°c for 5-10 minutes.

To serve: Lemon wedges and tartare sauce with chopped anchovies.

INGREDIENTS

Serves 4

400gms Salmon Fillet (free from skin and bone)
400g Cod Fillet (free from skin and bone)
4 heads Spring Onion (chopped)
50g Chopped Herbs (Chervil, Parsley and Tarragon)
100g (approx) Breadcrumbs
1-2 tbs Mayonnaise
Juice from ½ Lemon
Salt and Pepper
25g Flour
2 Beaten Eggs
20g Unsalted Butter
1 tbs Oil

182 - 186 Ocean Road, South Shields NE33 2JQ
Tel: 0191 456 1202, www.colmansfishandchips.com

Colman's
Est 1926

Colman's

SOUTH SHIELDS MUSSELS WITH TOMATO, CHORIZO AND FRESH BASIL

INGREDIENTS

Serves 4

- 1kg mussels with shells
- 30g butter
- A splash of olive oil
- 1 large tin of chopped tomatoes
- 2 garlic cloves, peeled and finely chopped
- A large sprig of fresh basil (chopped)
- 1 small chorizo sausage (diced in small cubes)
- 100ml good red wine

METHOD

For the mussels: Rinse the mussels under the tap, scrub the outside of the shells to clean and trim the hairy beard. Knock any open mussels hard with a implement (spoon/knife/fork). If they don't shut throw them out. Then wash again. There is one simple rule with mussels; when they are uncooked throw away any open mussels, when they are cooked throw away any that stay closed. As with any shellfish take particular care and attention in the cleaning and preparation of your mussels, if you have concerns at all always check with your fishmonger or shellfish supplier. Melt the butter gently in a pan large enough (with a lid) to hold the mussels. Add a generous splash of oil with the chorizo sausage and garlic fry on a medium heat for 5 munutes. Add the red wine and reduce by half. At this stage introduce the chopped tomatoes and fresh basil. As soon as the mixture is bubbling place the mussels in the pan gently and cover for three minutes or until all mussels have opened. Serve straight from the pan into a large bowl.

Garnish: With toasted crusty bread.

182 - 186 Ocean Road, South Shields NE33 2JQ
Tel: 0191 456 1202, www.colmansfishandchips.com

STIR-FRIED SQUID WITH GARLIC, CHILLI AND TOASTED SESAME SEEDS

METHOD

For the squid: Clean the squid and then cut along one side of each pouch and open out flat. Score the inner side into a diamond pattern with the tip of a small sharp knife, and then cut into 5cm (2 inch) squares. Separate the tentacles if large and set both to one side.

For garlic, chilli and sesame seeds: Put 6 tablespoons of oil into a small pan, when hot add chopped chilli and garlic. Fry for a few seconds, then remove chilli and garlic onto kitchen paper to remove excess oil (do not let the garlic go brown as this will give it a bitter taste). Heat a frying pan over a high heat, add sesame seeds and toast for a few seconds. Then remove from heat and set aside.

To finish squid: Heat a wok over a high heat until smoking, use 2 tablespoons of the oil from the chilli and garlic and add half the squid. Stir-fry for 2 minutes until lightly coloured. Tip onto a warm plate and repeat process with the rest of the squid. Place the squid on a warm serving plate, add a couple of turns of salt and black pepper, sprinkle over garlic, chilli, toasted sesame seeds, spring onion and coriander and finally finish with a squeeze of lime

To serve: Salad and lime wedges.

INGREDIENTS

Serves 4

- 750g fresh squid (unprepared)
- 2 medium hot red chillis (finely chopped)
- 3 garlic cloves (finely chopped)
- 1 teaspoon of toasted sesame seeds
- 3 spring onions (finely chopped)
- 2-3 fresh coriander sprigs (leaves and stalks, finely chopped)
- 6 tablespoons sunflower oil
- 1 lime
- Salt and black pepper

182 - 186 Ocean Road, South Shields NE33 2JQ
Tel: 0191 456 1202, www.colmansfishandchips.com

Colman's

CRAB & LOBSTER

Here at the Crab & Lobster we believe in homely, honest food served in comfortable surroundings with a modern European twist, nothing complicated just good food, simply but creatively cooked using the best produce of the day.

I have been Head Chef at the Crab & Lobster for over 17 years and I am extremely fortunate to have a well-established, dedicated team of chefs. This enables us to produce excellent food on a consistent basis.

With our enthusiastic staff and a network of exceptional local suppliers who fully understand our requirements, we have gone from strength to strength and continue to build on what has been achieved so far, I hope you will come along and enjoy trying our menu.

Stephen Dean, executive head chef

Crab Manor Hotel, Dishforth Road, Asenby, Thirsk, North Yorks YO7 3QL
Tel: 01845 577286, www.crabandlobster.co.uk

TART OF SEARED KING SCALLOPS WITH BLACK PUDDING, APPLE AND A BASIL DRESSING

METHOD

To prepare: Pre-heat oven to 200˚C.

For the pastry: Roll out to approximately 2mm thickness, prick all over with a fork and leave for 30 minutes. Cut the pastry into rectangles approximately 10cm x 6cm, place on a baking tray and bake for 7-8 minutes until lightly coloured.

For the apple puree: Peel, core and slice the apple and place in a pan with a tablespoon of water and a pinch of sugar. Cook gently until soft, blend to a puree and allow to cool.

For the basil dressing: Warm the oil and add to the fresh basil, seasoning, and 1/4 lemon juice, blend to a puree and allow to cool.

For the tart: Place a layer of apple puree on the part-baked pastry base, arrange sliced black pudding on the top and place in the oven for 5 minutes.

For the scallops: Once the tart is ready, cook the scallops in a little oil in a very hot frying pan for about 20-30 seconds until golden on each side, finish with the remaining lemon juice and butter.

To serve: Arrange the scallops neatly on top of the tart and serve on a warm plate drizzled with the basil dressing.

INGREDIENTS

Serves 4

- 12 king scallops
- 1 sheet of ready made puff pastry
- 4 x 75g black pudding pieces (sliced)
- 4 eating apples
- 50g fresh basil
- 4tbs extra virgin olive oil
- Juice of 1 lemon
- 50g unsalted butter
- Salt and pepper
- Sugar

Crab Manor Hotel, Dishforth Road, Asenby, Thirsk, North Yorks YO7 3QL
Tel: 01845 577286, www.crabandlobster.co.uk

SMOKED HADDOCK ON CHAMP WITH POACHED EGGS AND GRAIN MUSTARD SAUCE

INGREDIENTS

Serves 4

4 x 160g pieces of smoked haddock
12fl oz fish stock (see recipe below)
4fl oz dry white wine
10fl oz whipping cream
3tsp whole grain mustard
4 poached eggs
6 spring onions (sliced)
Salt and pepper
120g unsalted butter
1kg potatoes (boiling variety)

FISH STOCK

1kg white fish bones
1 litre water
1 onion
1 leek
1 lemon
Salt and pepper
2 bay leaves

METHOD

For the fish stock: Make in advance – wash the bones well in cold water, place all of the stock ingredients in a pan, bring to the boil and skim frequently. Simmer for 20 minutes then leave for 20 minutes. Strain through a fine sieve and allow to cool in the fridge.

For the champ: Peel and cut the potatoes into even sizes, place in a pan of salted water and boil until cooked. Drain well and return to the pan for 30 seconds to dry, mix in half of the butter and spring onions, season and keep warm.

For the fish: Place the wine and fish stock in a large pan, lay the smoked haddock side by side and simmer to poach for 4-5 minutes until cooked (it will be firm to touch). Remove the fish from the stock and keep warm, strain the stock and reduce quickly by two thirds, then add the cream and mustard until it starts to thicken.

For the eggs: Have a pan of boiling water ready to reheat the poached eggs in for 30 seconds.

To serve: Place the champ in a mound in the middle of a warmed plate, put the fish on top, then the drained poached egg. Pour the sauce over the egg and around the plate.

Crab Manor Hotel, Dishforth Road, Asenby, Thirsk, North Yorks YO7 3QL
Tel: 01845 577286, www.crabandlobster.co.uk

CRAB & LOBSTER

CHILLED LEMON SOUFFLÉ, SUMMER BERRIES AND SHORTBREAD

METHOD

To prepare: Tie a collar of baking paper around 4 individual ramekin dishes so that the paper is 2-4cms above top of the dish.

For the soufflé: Soak the gelatine leaves in cold water and put to one side. Put the egg yolks, lemon juice and zest in a large heat proof bowl. Bring a pan of water to the boil and turn off the heat. Place the bowl over the pan and whisk the mixture until pale. Heat 2 tablespoons of water, squeeze the excess water from soaked gelatine and dissolve in the hot water. Whisk into the lemon mixture and remove the bowl from the pan and set aside to cool. Whisk the egg whites in a clean bowl to soft peaks. In another bowl whisk the cream until thick, careful not to over whisk. Fold the cream into the lemon mixture, then carefully fold in the egg whites. Pour into the ramekin dishes and chill for at least 4 hours.

To serve: Carefully remove the paper by sliding a wet knife between the paper and soufflé mix. Serve with summer berries and shortbread.

INGREDIENTS

Serves 4

- 2 leaves of gelatine
- Zest and juice of 2 lemons
- 3 eggs (separated)
- 150g castor sugar
- 200ml whipping cream
- Summer berries
- Shortbread

Crab Manor Hotel, Dishforth Road, Asenby, Thirsk, North Yorks YO7 3QL
Tel: 01845 577286, www.crabandlobster.co.uk

EPICURUS

Events House, 5 Oslo Close, Tyne Tunnel Trading Estate, North Shields, NE29 7SZ, Tel: 0191 270 8540, www.epicurus.co.uk

epicurus

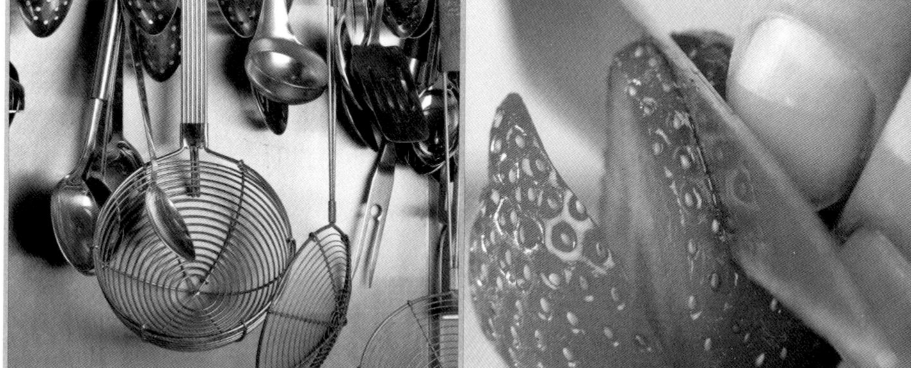

As we are event caterers and do not operate like a restaurant means we have to provide a vast range of different types and styles of food to suit our customers' requirements. This range includes finger food, canapés, bowl food, knife and fork buffets, BBQ's, and of course fine dining for events such as weddings and birthdays. One day we could be preparing canapés for 200 guests and the next we could be working on a wedding for 100 or a corporate dinner for 500 invited guests. Everyday is different for the team here! The fine dining is what we love to do the most as it allows us to work with some of the fantastic produce we have available here in the North East. All of our meat is sourced locally via our catering butcher, fish is from North Shields and our cream, eggs and cheeses all come from local farms. The business began in domestic premises back in 1998, but we now operate from a large purpose - built commercial kitchen situated in a warehouse near Newcastle. Our finished food is often served to guests in marquees, houses, castles and historic properties, from North Yorkshire up to the Borders and across into Cumbria.

Christopher Reay, MD and head chef

Events House, 5 Oslo Close, Tyne Tunnel Trading Estate, North Shields, NE29 7SZ
Tel: 0191 270 8540, www.epicurus.co.uk

EPICURUS

DOUBLE BAKED YORKSHIRE BLUE CHEESE SOUFFLÉ WITH RED ONION MARMALADE

METHOD

To prepare: Preheat the oven to 180°C and lightly butter 6 individual ramekins or dariole moulds and then line them with the breadcrumbs. Set aside in an oven tray.

For the soufflé: Heat the milk in a pan along with the bay leaf, onions, peppercorns and nutmeg until it simmers, then strain the milk into a jug.

Melt the remaining butter in a pan, add the flour and cook for a few minutes before gradually adding the strained milk whisking all the time. Season and cook for a couple of minutes until thick. Take off the heat and let it cool a little then slowly beat in the egg yolks one at a time, followed by the crumbled cheese, reserving a little for finishing. Whisk the egg whites until stiff then carefully fold in the cheese mixture making sure it is thoroughly mixed in. Divide between the moulds and top up the oven tray with boiling water to half way up the moulds.

To cook: Bake for about 20 minutes then transfer to a cooling rack. Once they are cool tip them out of the moulds and then place them (right side up) on a lined oven tray ready for cooking (you can do this the day before and chill them if required).

To finish: Bake in the oven again with the remaining cheese sprinkled on the top for about 30-40 minutes until they are well risen and golden.

To serve: Serve with red onion marmalade, salad & walnut oil.

INGREDIENTS

Serves 6

- 175g Yorkshire blue cheese (crumbled)
- 225ml milk
- 1 bay leaf
- 1 grating of nutmeg
- 6 whole black peppercorns
- 50g unsalted butters (softened)
- 50g plain flour
- 6 free range eggs (separated)
- 2 slices white bread (made into breadcrumbs)
- 1/2 small onion (sliced)
- salt and pepper

Events House, 5 Oslo Close, Tyne Tunnel Trading Estate, North Shields NE29 7SZ
Tel: 0191 270 8540, www.epicurus.co.uk

ROASTED RUMP OF INGRAM VALLEY LAMB STUFFED WITH MUSHROOM, TRUFFLE AND PINE NUTS

INGREDIENTS

Serves 6

- 6 potions of lamb rump
- 100g mushroom & truffle paste
- 75g pine nuts
- 2 tbs rosemary (chopped)
- 2 tbs thyme (chopped)
- 2 tbs mint (chopped)
- 3 cloves of garlic (chopped)
- 6 large Yukon Gold potatoes
- 50g butter
- 500ml vegetable stock
- sprig of thyme
- salt and pepper

METHOD

To prepare: Preheat the oven to 190˚C.

For the stuffing: Miix together the truffle paste, pine nuts, garlic and herbs and pulse in a blender for a few seconds and spoon into a piping bag.

For the lamb: Cut a pocket into each of the lamb rumps and carefully pipe in some of the truffle mixture and season with salt and pepper.

To cook: Seal the lamb in a hot, oiled pan and then place in the oven for 15-20 minutes (for pink or longer if preferred). Remove and allow to rest.

For the fondant potatoes: Cut the potatoes into cylindrical shapes using a pastry cutter or fondant potato cutter. Place in an oven tray and almost cover with the stock, along with the thyme and butter. Cook for about 25 minutes until the stock has evaporated and the top of the potato is golden brown. Brush periodically with melted butter. Season before serving.

To serve: Sice the lamb and arrange on the plate with the potato and serve with a red wine sauce.

Events House, 5 Oslo Close, Tyne Tunnel Trading Estate, North Shields NE29 7SZ
Tel: 0191 270 8540, www.epicurus.co.uk

LINDISFARNE MEAD PARFAIT WITH BAKED BLACKBERRIES

METHOD

To prepare: Using a round 75mm dessert mould, stamp out 6 pieces of sponge leaving them inside the moulds (these will form the base of the dessert).

For the parfait: Whisk the egg yolks until they turn thick and ribbon like. Mix together the water and sugar in a pan and boil until it reaches 120˚C on a sugar thermometer. Immediately pour onto the egg mixture whilst whisking at the same time. Set the bowl over some cold water to cool the mixture. Whip up the vanilla seeds, cream and mead into soft peaks, then carefully fold into the cooled syrup mixture. Pour into the dessert moulds and smooth of the top with a palette knife. Freeze overnight and then remove from the dessert rings by heating lightly with a cooks blowtorch and tapping them out of the ring. Place them back in the freezer until required.

To finish: Place the blackberries in an oven dish and put in a hot oven for about 5 minutes. Remove the desserts from the freezer, dust the tops with cocoa powder and serve with the baked blackberries.

INGREDIENTS

Serves 6

- 100ml Lindisfarne mead
- 3 egg yolks
- 175g castor sugar
- 350ml double cream
- 1 vanilla pod (seeds scraped out)
- 100ml water
- cocoa powder (for dusting)
- 250g blackberries
- mint (to garnish)
- sponge base

Events House, 5 Oslo Close, Tyne Tunnel Trading Estate, North Shields NE29 7SZ
Tel: 0191 270 8540, www.epicurus.co.uk

ESLINGTON VILLA

8 Station Road, Low Fell, Gateshead NE9 6DR Tel: 0191 487 6017, www.eslingtonvilla.co.uk

VILLA
HOTEL

For the past 22 years we have owned and run this hidden gem of a restaurant. Eslington Villa is tucked away from the bright lights of the city, in two acres of gardens in a quiet, leafy part of Low Fell, Gateshead.

Stepping into Eslington Villa is like stepping into the home of an old friend. Our beautiful Victorian restaurant and hotel combines wonderful original features with a comfortable and stylish interior to create the ideal atmosphere for enjoying our outstanding and award-winning dining. We believe that good quality ingredients speak for themselves. We produce simple, stylish yet innovative dishes made from the very best seasonal and regional produce. We live in a region where a fantastic larder of ingredients is on our doorstep and these are the cornerstones of our cooking. However, this doesn't mean that you won't find ingredients from other countries or cuisines; we also like to keep abreast of international food trends and techniques and our chef Andy Moore incorporates elements of these into our classic style. We think that we have produced something very special at Eslington Villa, the very best in food and drink in a relaxed, friendly and unpretentious atmosphere created by our small, family-led team. The comfort and satisfaction of our customers is at the heart of everything we do; this is why we have many customers who have been returning for almost as many years as we have been here.

Nick and Melanie Tulip, owners

8 Station Road, Low Fell, Gateshead NE9 6DR
Tel: 0191 487 6017, www.eslingtonvilla.co.uk

SLOW COOKED CHICKEN AND HAM TERRINE

METHOD

To prepare: Pre heat the oven to 140˚C.

For the terrine: Place the chopped onions in a pan and cover with the white wine, bring to the boil then simmer and reduce until the onions are tender and the mixture is almost dry. Set aside and allow to cool down thoroughly. In a bowl, mix all of the chopped meats, herbs, cooled onions, beaten egg yolks, and season generously with black pepper and a couple of pinches of salt. Line the terrine mould with a double layer of cling film and place the streaky bacon in a layer, overlapping and covering the inside of the mould. Place the mixture inside and push down firmly to fill all corners. Wrap any bacon left hanging over the top of the terrine and bang the terrine firmly on the bench to release any air.

To cook: Cover the top with cling film and foil. Place in a roasting tray filled halfway with water and place in the pre-heated oven. Cook for between 1-2 hours until the terrine is piping hot in the centre – check by using a metal skewer every 15 minutes once the terrine has been in for an hour. Take out and leave on a rack, lightly weighed down, until cooled.

To serve: Turn out and serve sliced at room temperature with dressed mixed leaves and gherkins.

INGREDIENTS

Serves 10

- 300g pork belly (roughly diced)
- 600g chicken breast (finely chopped or minced)
- 3 chicken breasts (skin removed and roughly chopped)
- 3 medium gammon steaks (skin removed and sliced)
- 2 large white onions (finely chopped)
- 300ml white wine
- 3 tbs chopped herbs (sage, tarragon, parsley and chives)
- 12 slices streaky bacon
- 3 free range egg yolks
- salt and pepper
- mixed leaves
- gherkins

8 Station Road, Low Fell, Gateshead NE9 6DR
Tel: 0191 487 6017, www.eslingtonvilla.co.uk

DUCK – TWO WAYS

INGREDIENTS

Serves 4

- 2 duck breasts
- 2 duck legs
- 1kg duck fat (melted)
- 4 tbs sea salt
- 2 cloves of garlic (finely chopped)
- 1 tbs chopped fresh thyme
- 6 large potatoes (peeled)
- 250g butter
- 1 litre chicken stock
- 6 banana shallots (finely sliced)
- 200g button mushrooms (sliced)
- 50ml port
- ½ bottle red wine
- 2 litres brown chicken or veal stock
- 500g swede (peeled and chopped)
- 4 sticks of salsify
- juice of 1 lemon
- 1 bag of baby spinach
- butter
- salt and pepper

METHOD

To prepare: 24 hours before, mix the salt, garlic and thyme together and scatter over the duck legs in a shallow dish and place in the fridge overnight. For the duck, the next day, wash the duck legs thoroughly and pat dry. Place in an ovenproof dish with the duck fat and put in a pre-heated oven at 140°C for 2½ hours. Take out of the fat and allow to cool. For the potatoes, with a small metal pastry cutter cut cylindrical shapes out of each potato. Thinly slice the butter and line the bottom of a pan. Place the potatoes on top and cover with the chicken stock. Bring to the boil and simmer for 10-15 minutes until the stock evaporates and caramelises the potatoes.

For the sauce: In a heavy bottomed pan, melt a knob of butter and add the shallots and mushrooms, sweat down and colour a little. Add the port and red wine and reduce until almost dry. Add the stock, bring to the boil and simmer for 30 minutes or until a sauce consistency is reached, then strain.

For the vegetables: Boil the swede until tender. Drain and place in a food processor with seasoning and blend until smooth. Add a little butter. Wash and peel the salsify in lemon water. Blanch in boiling water for two minutes and refresh in cold water. Cut into strips and then set aside to sauté just prior to serving.

For the duck: Cut the duck legs in half and place on a non-stick tray skin side down and put in a pre heated oven to 180°C for 15-20 minutes until crisp. Heat a frying pan and place the duck breasts skin side down and cook for 2 minutes each side, then place in the oven for 5 minutes, remove and allow to rest. Cut each breast in two diagonally.

To serve: Sauté the salsify, wilt the spinach in a pan, remove excess water, lightly season and add some butter. On each plate serve half a duck leg and breast, with the salsify, spinach, potatoes and red wine sauce.

8 Station Road, Low Fell, Gateshead NE9 6DR
Tel: 0191 487 6017, www.eslingtonvilla.co.uk

WHITE CHOCOLATE FONDANT WITH DARK CHOCOLATE CENTRE

METHOD

To prepare: Grease and flour the dariole moulds and pre-heat the oven to 180˚C.

For the centre: Put a non-stick pan on a low heat until warm then remove, add the dark chocolate buttons and stir with a wooden spoon to slowly melt the chocolate, add the Grand Marnier and chilled double cream. Continue stirring until it starts to form ribbons. Pour into an ice cube tray and freeze for at least 2 hours.

For the fondant: Melt together the white chocolate buttons and butter in a bowl over a pan of hot water. When melted and glossy, remove from the heat and allow to cool a little. Whisk together the eggs, yolks and sugar until trebled in volume. Carefully fold in the sifted flour. Make sure the mixture is well combined and then add the white chocolate mix to the egg and flour mix. Evenly fill the moulds until almost full and chill in the fridge for an hour. Push a chocolate ice cube into the centre of each dessert and place the moulds on an oven tray and bake for 11 minutes.

For the chocolate sauce: Break the dark chocolate into pieces and place in a bowl. Pour over 200ml boiling water and place the bowl over another bowl containing iced water. Whisk until it resembles whipped double cream.

To serve: Turn out of the moulds and serve straight away with the sauce and a garnish of raspberries.

INGREDIENTS

Serves 4-6

- 200g dark chocolate buttons
- 20ml Grand Marnier (or good quality whisky)
- 180ml double cream (chilled)
- 250g white chocolate buttons
- 250g unsalted butter
- 5 medium egg yolks
- 5 medium eggs
- 125g castor sugar
- 145g plain flour
- 200g of dark chocolate (70 cocoa solids)
- 200ml boiling water
- small punnet of raspberries

8 Station Road, Low Fell, Gateshead NE9 6DR
Tel: 0191 487 6017, www.eslingtonvilla.co.uk

THE FEATHERS INN

Hedley On The Hill, Northumberland, NE43 7SW, Tel: 01661 843 607, www.thefeathers.net

France, Picpoul de Pinet
Juicy, fruit driven & ripe
Australia, Riesling, Stonehaven 2005
Australia, Chardonnay, Firefly 2007
Italy, Chardonnay, Distinto 2006
Full flavoured, nutty & oaked
Argentina, Pinot Gris, Bodega Lurton 2007
16.00/4.40
13.00/3.60
12.00/3.30
18.00/4.95
Champagne & fizz
House Champagne
Piper Hiedsieck
Veuve Cliquot
Perrier Jouet Belle Epoque '98
Three Chairs English Fizz
Cremant de Bourgogne rosé
Ebe prosecco
Spain, Rioja Joven
South Africa, Pinotage, Kleine Zalze
Chile, Carmenère, Indomita 2007
Oaked, Intense & concentrated
Lebanon, Chateau Musar 2001
Rosé Wines
2007
Spain, Tempranillo, Reinares
Italy, Bardolino, Bolla 2007
Dessert Wines/Liqueur
France, Golden & rich, Monbazillac
Spain, Spiced brandy, Ponche Caballero
California, Black muscat, Elysium
THE FEATHERS INN
THE GOOD PUB GUIDE 2009
THE GOOD FOOD GUIDE 2009
Taste of Britain
FOOD MANIA
COOKING for KINGS
LAROUSSE

THE FEATHERS INN

Over two centuries old and still at the heart of the community, The Feathers Inn, Hedley on the Hill, lies on the old drovers' road between Hadrian's Wall and the beautiful Derwent Valley. The imaginative and delicious menu at the Feathers changes twice daily to incorporate the freshest of local ingredients. The aim is to embrace the flavours of the region and to evoke British classics. Award-winning chef and owner Rhian Cradock works to create these dishes with passion, celebrating the finest produce of the North East.

The menu includes rare breed local highland cattle, homemade black pudding, wild salmon from the South Tyne and game from local shoots. You can enjoy one of several cask ales beside a real open fire, and pick up one of the many cookery books that fill the shelves. The Feathers Inn and its inspiring Northumbrian views make it the perfect venue for a relaxing afternoon lunch, meeting with friends or an intimate dinner. With regular farmers' markets and village events, a warm and friendly environment will ensure a memorable experience.

You can visit The Feathers Inn from Monday 6pm until 11pm and from Tuesday to Saturday 12pm until 11pm. Sunday opening is 12pm until 10.30pm. Lunch is served on Tuesday to Saturday from 12pm until 2pm and on Sunday from 12pm until 2.30pm. Dinner is Tuesday to Saturday 6pm until 8.30pm.

Rhian and his wife Helen, along with their fantastic team of staff, look forward to welcoming you to The Feathers Inn very soon.

Helen and Rhian Cradock, proprietors

Hedley On The Hill, Northumberland, NE43 7SW
Tel: 01661 843 607, www.thefeathers.net

HOLY ISLAND MUSSELS IN CIDER

METHOD

Steve Oldale hand collects wild mussels from the beautiful coastline of Holy island. He processes them by hand and delivers them the next day to the Feathers. They are by far the freshest and tastiest mussels I've ever had, with generous orange meats in salty and sweet liquor.

For the mussels: Before cooking, discard any open or cracked specimens as well as any that don't close when tapped. It's rare that I discard any of Steve's mussels.

To prepare: If you are using Holy Island mussels, as they are not processed in fresh water they need to be steamed open in a dry pan with a tight fitting lid over a high heat for a couple of minutes. Throw the liquor they produce away as it is very salty. If you are not using Holy Island mussels then you can skip this first step. Place the mussels in a pan with of all the ingredients except the parsley, bring them to a rapid boil and cook until the mussels are fully open.

To serve: season the sauce, add the parsley and serve immediately with crusty bread.

INGREDIENTS

Serves 4

- 1.5kg Holy Island mussels
- 3 cloves of garlic (roughly chopped)
- 1 shallot (roughly chopped)
- large bunch of parsley leaves (roughly chopped)
- 250ml dry cider (we use a Cumbrian cider called Rock Robin)
- 100ml Northumbrian double cream
- Salt and black pepper (to season)

Hedley On The Hill, Northumberland, NE43 7SW
Tel: 01661 843 607, www.thefeathers.net

JUGGED HARE WITH FRIED BREAD, FORCEMEAT BALLS AND REDCURRANT JELLY

INGREDIENTS

Serves 8-10

- 1 large hare (skinned and gutted)
- 4 shallots (roughly chopped)
- 2 carrots (peeled and roughly chopped)
- 4 sticks of celery (stringed and chopped)
- 200g of dry-cured streaky (cut in to 1cm cubes)
- Plain flour
- Ground mace
- Nutmeg
- Bunch of fresh herbs (bay, rosemary, thyme and parsley stalks)
- 2 garlic cloves (peeled)
- 250ml port
- 250ml red wine
- 50g red currant jelly (with extra to serve)

FORCEMEAT BALLS:

- 200g shredded suet
- 400g fresh white breadcrumbs
- Zest of 1 lemon (finely grated)
- 2 eggs
- 2tbs parsley (finely chopped)
- 1 litre of beef or chicken stock

METHOD

To start: Joint hare into two legs, cut saddle into three pieces and split the shoulder. Refrigerate any blood with a splash of red wine. Soak the offal in milk for the forcemeat balls. Mix salt, pepper, mace and nutmeg with enough plain flour to coat the hare, fry coated hare over a moderate heat until evenly browned. Drain and set aside. In the same pan fry the shallots, carrots, celery and bacon until browned and fat released. Return hare to pan, add wine, port, herbs and garlic, season, cover with stock and place in low to medium oven for 3 hours. Remove hare from pan and strain through colander to discard vegetables and keep liquor. This may be done in advance, keeping any liquor in fridge until ready to serve.

For the forcemeat balls: Place the offal from the hare on paper towels to soak the milk, season with salt and fry over a brisk heat until brown, but still pink. Add half a finely chopped shallot, then deglaze with a splash of brandy and port. Tip the offal mixture into a food processor and pulse chop roughly. Combine with the rest of the ingredients, adding a little water if necessary, into a soft pliable dough. Roll into walnut-sized pieces and fry in hot oil until brown and crisp. Served with the hare and the redcurrant jelly, adding some slices of fried bread on the side.

To serve: Return liquor to heat and without boiling add any blood and allow sauce to thicken. Return hare to pan to warm through and serve.

Hedley On The Hill, Northumberland, NE43 7SW
Tel: 01661 843 607, www.thefeathers.net

HEDGEROW FRUIT SPONGE WITH ELDERFLOWER CUSTARD

METHOD

To start: Stew the fruit. Start with the damsons and cook until they are soft. Then add the blackberries and elderberries as they take less time to cook. Add sugar and lemon juice to taste. Place all the sponge ingredients in a food processor and blend until thoroughly incorporated adding a little milk until it reaches dropping consistency. Butter four individual pudding moulds, place a tablespoon of the cooled fruit mixture into the bottom of each mould, then fill up with the sponge mixture till two thirds full. Steam in a basket over boiling water for 35 minutes until the sponge mixture is cooked. Turn off heat and allow to rest in hot pan while you make the custard.

For the custard: Bring the milk and cream to the boil in a large pan with the vanilla pod and elderflower blooms. Set aside and leave to infuse for ten minutes. Whisk the sugar and yolks until thick and creamy and doubled in volume. Bring the milk and cream back to the boil and sieve into the yolk mixture. Place back into a clean pan and cook over gentle heat until thickened. Turn out the sponges and serve with the custard on the side. Feel free to drizzle any leftover stewed fruit on the side.

INGREDIENTS

Serves 4

250g blackberries, elderberries and damsons (de-stoned)
150g caster sugar
Squeeze of lemon juice

SPONGE:
250g soft butter
4 eggs
250g self-raising flour
250g caster sugar
A little milk

CUSTARD:
250ml whole milk
250ml double cream
1 vanilla pod (split, seeds scraped out and put into milk)
125g caster sugar
6 egg yolks
6 large elderflower blooms (washed) or 1 tbs elderflower cordial

Hedley On The Hill, Northumberland, NE43 7SW
Tel: 01661 843 607, www.thefeathers.net

GREEN'S

13 Bridge Street, Whitby, North Yorkshire YO22 4BG, Tel: 01947 600 284, www.greensofwhitby.com

WHITBY
WHITBY

Being passionate about seafood has been made easy for me, living and working in Whitby for nearly 20 years. The fish quay is a stone's throw away from Green's and we take full advantage of this.

Our food is fresh, extremely local, and cooked simply using modern techniques to let the main ingredients shine.This year has been made even more special after receiving the coverted ' seafood chef of the year' award by the Sea fish Authority.

With passion, hard work and great relationships with our fantastic suppliers we hope to maintain the very high standards of quality that our customers demand for yet another year.

Rob Green, chef and proprietor

13 Bridge Street, Whitby, North Yorkshire YO22 4BG
Tel: 01947 600 284, www.greensofwhitby.com

WHITBY QUEEN SCALLOPS WITH SLEIGHTS AIR DRIED HAM, PESTO AND PARMESAN

METHOD

To Start: Pre heat your grill to full.

For the scallops: Place a little of each of the ham, pesto and parmesan on each of the scallops in the shell. Place under the hot grill and cook for two mins only until the ham starts to crisp and the parmesan starts to melt.

To serve: Serve straight away scattered with baby herbs.

INGREDIENTS

Serves 4

40 Queen scallops in the half shell, cleaned and skirt removed (if unsure ask your fishmonger to help)

2 slices of cured Sleights ham (or Parma ham) thinly sliced

25g fresh grated parmesan

200ml fresh pesto (preferably homemade)

13 Bridge Street, Whitby, North Yorkshire YO22 4BG
Tel: 01947 600 284, www.greensofwhitby.com

WHITBY HALIBUT WITH SPROUTING BROCCOLI, MUSSELS, ORANGE CREAM AND A SPRING ONION AND KING PRAWN FRITTER

INGREDIENTS

Serves 4

- 4x 200g thick fillets of halibut
- 20 sprouting broccoli
- 12 live mussels, cleaned
- 200ml fresh squeezed orange juice
- 200ml cream
- 100ml chicken stock
- 4x large raw tiger prawn tails, chopped
- 2 spring onions, chopped
- 2 eggs
- 75g self raising flour
- 25g melted butter
- 100ml milk

METHOD

For the sauce: Reduce the orange juice and stock by half in a saucepan over a high heat, add the cream and bring to the boil, keep warm.

For the fritter: Mix the eggs, milk and flour together to form a smooth batter add the prawns, spring onions and seasoning, mix well. Using a dessert spoon carefully drop a spoon full of mixture into hot oil (180˚C) and cook until golden brown, keep warm.

For the halibut: Season each halibut fillet and pan fry in a little olive oil until coloured on all sides. Place in a hot oven to finish cooking (5-8mins depending on thickness of fillets).

For the sprouting broccoli: Cook the broccoli in boiling salted water and steam open the mussels.

To serve: Place the broccoli on the warmed plates with the halibut on top. Put the mussels around the fish and top with the fritter. Pour the sauce around and garnish with a few orange segments.

13 Bridge Street, Whitby, North Yorkshire YO22 4BG
Tel: 01947 600 284, www.greensofwhitby.com

GREEN'S

WHITE CHOCOLATE MOUSSE WITH CHOCOLATE CHIP SHORTBREAD

METHOD

For the mousse: Whip the cream to soft peaks. Break the white chocolate into small pieces. Bring the water and glucose to the boil and add the gelatine and chocolate, mix until smooth. When cool add the egg yolks and fold in the cream. Pour or pipe into suitable moulds / glasses

For the biscuits: Pre heat oven to 180 gas 4. Cream the butter and sugar together. Sift the flours together and work into the butter mix. Pipe the mix onto a baking sheet into desired shapes and bake in the oven for 20mins

To serve: Place the mousse on a plate with the biscuits and serve with some fresh raspberries and a little raspberry sorbet.

INGREDIENTS

Serves 4

MOUSSE:

- 2 gelatine leaves soaked and ready for use
- 600ml double cream
- 275g white chocolate
- 50ml water
- 2 tablespoons liquid glucose
- 2 egg yolks

BISCUITS:

- 225g unsalted butter
- 75g caster sugar
- 450g plain flour
- 15g cornflour
- 25g plain or milk chocolate broken into small pieces

13 Bridge Street, Whitby, North Yorkshire YO22 4BG
Tel: 01947 600 284, www.greensofwhitby.com

HORTON GRANGE COUNTRY HOUSE HOTEL & RESTAURANT

Berwick Hill Road, Ponteland, Newcastle upon Tyne NE13 6BU, Tel: 01661 860686, www.hortongrange.co.uk

Horton Grange Country House Hotel & Restaurant is situated on the Blagdon Estate, three miles east of Ponteland, and seven miles from Newcastle city centre. This elegant and intimate Grade-II listed country house has a distinctive mix of traditional and contemporary décor, and is set in four acres of beautiful grounds. Horton Grange offers nine spacious en-suite bedrooms all individually furnished and decorated. The dining room creates a relaxed atmosphere overlooking the glorious gardens, offering the increasingly rare opportunity to relax and enjoy the freshest of culinary delights. Our head chef, Barry Forster, uses only the very best fresh local produce to create an imaginative modern-classic a la carte menu with a range of exciting dishes to suit all tastes. From a light lunch to a four-course dinner, we guarantee our guests a gastronomic experience only enhanced by a wine list of great distinction. Horton Grange Country House Hotel & Restaurant is the perfect venue for everyday dining, private functions, weddings and special occasions, and we look forward to welcoming you soon.

Alistair Mathieson, general manager

Berwick Hill Road, Ponteland, Newcastle upon Tyne NE13 6BU
Tel: 01661 860686, www.hortongrange.co.uk

RAVIOLI OF LOBSTER

METHOD

For the pasta dough: Put the flour, salt and olive oil into a food processor and blitz. Add the eggs and additional egg yolks and blend until the pasta begins to come together. Knead the dough well on a flat surface. Cut into 2 pieces, wrap in cling film and rest in the refrigerator for 20 minutes.

For the filling: Blanche the lobster in rapidly boiling water for 3 minutes. Take out and leave it to cool. Remove the flesh from the claws and tail and chop roughly. Fold together with the cream, chives and lemon juice and season to taste.

For the ravioli: Roll the pasta very thinly, preferably through a pasta machine. Cut into discs approximately 7cm in diameter. Place a small amount of filling in the centre. Brush the edges with egg wash and place another disc on top and very carefully shape into neat parcels. Cook in boiling, salted water for 3 minutes.

For the lobster sauce: Fry the lobster shell and onions gently for 5 minutes in the olive oil. Add the brandy, tomato purée and white wine and bring to the boil. Add the double cream and simmer for 15 minutes. Pass through a sieve and season to taste.

To serve: Serve the ravioli dressed with the lobster sauce.

INGREDIENTS

Serves 4

PASTA DOUGH

250g plain flour
Salt
Olive oil
2 eggs
3 egg yolks
1 egg yolk with a drop of water (egg wash)

RAVIOLI FILLING

1 small lobster
100ml cream (lightly whipped)
Lemon juice
Chives
Salt and pepper

LOBSTER SAUCE

1 lobster shell (chopped finely)
2 onions (finely diced)
1 tbs tomato purée
50ml brandy
100ml white wine
100ml double cream
2 tbs olive oil

Berwick Hill Road, Ponteland, Newcastle upon Tyne NE13 6BU
Tel: 01661 860686, www.hortongrange.co.uk

TRUFFLE STUFFED ROAST ORGANIC CHICKEN

INGREDIENTS

Serves 4

ROAST CHICKEN

- 1.5kg organic chicken
- 1 small fresh or tinned block truffle
- 125g unsalted butter (soft)
- Olive oil
- Salt and pepper

FONDANT POTATOES

- 1kg maris piper potatoes
- 250g unsalted butter

STUFFED CHERRY TOMATOES

- 12 cherry tomatoes
- 100g button mushrooms (very finely chopped)
- 50g butter
- 1/2 onion (very finely diced)

VEGETABLES

- 4 portions fine beans
- 4 portions young turnips
- 4 portions baby carrots

METHOD

To prepare: Pre-heat the oven to 180˚C.

For the chicken: Mix the soft butter with the chopped truffle. Spread the mixture under the skin of the chicken breast. Brush the chicken with oil and season. Roast for approximately 1 hour until golden brown and the juices run clear.

For the potatoes: Peel and cut the potatoes into 3cm cubes. Melt the butter in an oven-proof pan, add the potatoes and brown gently. Put the pan in the oven and cook at 180°C for approximately 30 minutes or until the potatoes are cooked and have absorbed all of the butter.

For the tomatoes: Gently fry the onion in the butter, add the mushrooms and cook for 10 minutes on a gentle heat, season with salt and pepper. Carefully cut the tops off the tomatoes and scoop out the seeds. Fill the tomato shells with the mushroom mixture and put the tops back on. Bake in the oven for 5 minutes at 180˚C.

For the accompanying vegetables: Cook separately in boiling, salted water for approximately 5 minutes or until tender. Toss in melted butter and season before serving.

Berwick Hill Road, Ponteland, Newcastle upon Tyne NE13 6BU
Tel: 01661 860686, www.hortongrange.co.uk

CHOCOLATE FONDANT PUDDING

METHOD

To prepare: Pre-heat the oven to 180˚C, and butter five individual pudding bowls, dust with flour and sugar.

For the pudding: Melt the butter and the chocolate in a bowl on top of a pan of hot water. Whilst this is melting, whisk the eggs, yolks and sugar together. When the chocolate and butter has melted whisk this into the egg mixture, then fold in the flour. Bake at 180˚C for 7 minutes.

To serve: Serve immediately with a good quality ice cream.

INGREDIENTS

Serves 5

- 150g good quality dark chocolate
- 150g unsalted butter
- 2 eggs
- 2 egg yolks
- 15g flour
- 60g caster sugar
- Spare butter, flour and sugar to line the bowls
- Ice cream (to serve)

Berwick Hill Road, Ponteland, Newcastle upon Tyne NE13 6BU
Tel: 01661 860686, www.hortongrange.co.uk

PAN HAGGERTY

At Pan Haggerty restaurant, Newcastle we are one of the few venues in the City that is fiercely proud of our traditional North East roots. Based on Newcastle's bustling Quayside, our innovative restaurant creates hearty dishes and rustic British cuisine in warm, yet chic surroundings. The relaxed and informal atmosphere along with the central riverside location makes Pan Haggerty an idyllic setting to spend an afternoon or evening and has sparked a high amount of interest from individuals, keen to taste our array of home cooking.

After working at McCoy's at the BALTIC, I hoped to bring success to Pan Haggerty with no nonsense food and skills which I had gained from my 20 year career in the food business. My passion for traditional British dishes has allowed Pan Haggerty to break through the formal restaurant conventions and distinguishes itself from other establishments in the area. Pan Haggerty's hearty portions and familiar recipes attract visitors from around the region. The ever-changing menu consists of timeless classics suitable for lunch and evening meals, guaranteeing that there will be something to suit everyone's palate.

Owners, Mike Morley and Craig Potts have worked endlessly to define the restaurant as one which provides indulgent, quality food. The combination of locally sourced ingredients and value for money prices enables visitors to regain their enthusiasm for British cuisine. This vision makes Pan Haggerty a suitable location for any event, from Sunday lunch with family to an exclusive business meal and has earned us the Best New Restaurant Award at the annual Gourmet Society's North East Restaurant Awards 2009.

Simon Wood, head chef

21 Queen Street, Newcastle, NE1 3UG
Tel: 0191 221 0904, www.panhaggerty.com

BACON FLODDIE

METHOD

For the floddie: Grate the potatoes and then squeeze in a towel to remove excess liquid. Grill the bacon and slice thinly. In a mixing bowl combine the potato, bacon, cheese, egg and thyme and season well. Heat a small pan and then add oil. Add the mixture and fry until golden turn over and cook for a further 2 minutes.

For the sauce: Add the vinegar, shallots and pepper to a pan and heat until reduced by half. In a separate bowl add lemon juice, egg yolks and a pinch of salt and pepper. Slowly add the reduction and whisk together for approximately 10 minutes, before placing over a bain-marie and continuing to whisk to form a thick foam. Remove from the heat and gradually whisk in small quantities of butter. Season to taste and sharpen with a squeeze of lemon if necessary.

To serve: Place the floddie on the plate, add a soft poached egg and pan fried black pudding on top, drizzle over the hollandaise sauce and garnish with crispy bacon.

INGREDIENTS

Serves 4

FLODDIE:

- 4 large potatoes (peeled)
- 3 rashers of smoked bacon
- 200g smoked cheese (grated)
- 1 tsp picked thyme
- 1 egg
- Salt and pepper

HOLLANDAISE SAUCE:

- 100ml white wine vinegar
- 1 shallot (finely chopped)
- 10 crushed white peppercorns
- 50ml cold water
- 1 tbs white wine
- 2 egg yolks
- 250g butter (clarified)
- Juice from 1/2 a lemon
- Salt and pepper

21 Queen Street, Newcastle, NE1 3UG
Tel: 0191 221 0904, www.panhaggerty.com

ROAST LOIN OF RABBIT WITH PAN HAGGERTY AND BARLEY STEW

INGREDIENTS

Serves 4

4 large potatoes (peeled)
100g cheese (grated)
1 large onion
1 tsp picked thyme
Salt and pepper
75g unsalted butter

BARLEY STEW:

150g barley
50g onion (diced)
50g carrot (diced)
30g celery (diced)
1 rasher of bacon (chopped)
50g wild mushrooms
400 ml of vegetable stock
Salt and pepper

RABBIT:

1 rabbit loin (boned out)
1 tsp shallots (finely chopped)
½ clove garlic
50g wild mushrooms
1 leaf of wild garlic
2 rashers of streaky bacon
Salt and pepper

METHOD

To start: Finely slice the potatoes and onions and then line a small roasting tray with grease proof paper. Layer the tray, starting with the potatoes, sprinkle the cheese over the top and then layer the onions and add the thyme and seasoning. Repeat the process until the tray is full. Dice the butter into cubes and place on top of the layers. Cover the tray with another sheet of grease proof paper and bake in a 150° preheated oven for 15-20 minutes. Remove from the oven when golden, leave to cool and then slice into individual portions.

For the stew: Heat a sauce pan with a little oil then add the vegetables and bacon and fry for a minute. Add the barley to the pan and then slowly ladle in the vegetable stock, seasoning at the same time. Continue to add the vegetable stock until the barley is cooked through.

For the rabbit: Heat a saucepan and gently fry the shallots, garlic and mushrooms until tender, season and then remove from the heat and leave to cool. Open the rabbit out and then place the wild garlic down the centre of the rabbit loin and add the shallot and mushroom mix. Roll the rabbit in the streaky bacon and wrap in cling film and poach in boiling water for 2 minutes. Remove from cling film and fry in hot oil until golden brown.

To serve: Place the pan haggerty on the dish, spoon the barley stew onto the plate and place the sliced rabbit loin over the top. Add the braised shallots and sautéed wild mushrooms to finish the dish.

21 Queen Street, Newcastle, NE1 3UG
Tel: 0191 221 0904, www.panhaggerty.com

PAN HAGGERTY

SINGING HINNIES WITH LEMON CURD AND WILD STRAWBERRY ICE CREAM

METHOD

For the hinnies: Add the flour, butter and lard to a bowl and mix together by hand. Add the salt, baking powder and currants. Pour in a small amount of milk and mix until bound together into a soft dough. Roll into small balls and flatten to approximately 1cm depth. Cook in a hot, dry pan until golden brown on each side.

For the lemon curd: Grate rind of the lemons and squeeze out the juice into a heatproof bowl. Add the sugar, butter and beaten eggs and place on top of a pan of boiling water. Stir with a wooden spoon until thick and curd coats the back of the spoon. Pour into a container, cover and place in fridge to cool.

To serve: Place singing hinnies on a plate, drizzle over lemon curd and add one scoop of Wheelbirks strawberry ice cream.

INGREDIENTS

Serves 4

HINNIES:

- 450g plain flour
- 40g butter
- 40g lard
- 20g currants
- 1/2 tsp salt
- 1 tsp baking powder
- Splash of milk

LEMON CURD:

- 4 lemons (including rind and juice)
- 4 eggs
- 110g butter
- 450g sugar

21 Queen Street, Newcastle, NE1 3UG
Tel: 0191 221 0904, www.panhaggerty.com

FILINI

OLIVE
OIL

LIVESTRONG

Filini is a contemporary Italian bar and restaurant. At Filini, we serve straightforward simply cooked Italian food based on carefully chosen ingredients. The setting is smart and modern – and the service is friendly, fast paced and unpretentious.

Filini is all about taste and flavour. Much time is put in to gathering the very best ingredients from Italy and its many regions – and we place great importance on not substituting with inferior products.

Filini has a strong wine culture and the wine selection is a highly visible feature at the restaurant. The wines are from various winemaking regions of Italy, all chosen to compliment the taste and flavours of the extensive menu.

Filini Bar is ideal to lounge and pose in. Coffee, aperitif, or just a drink – whatever your heart's desire, at Filini we promise to satisfy it.

Filini seeks to make an impact on all the senses. The food, the ingredients, the staff, the service, the surroundings and the ambience all help to make up the experience. You'll find us at the Radisson BLU hotel, Durham.

Rhys Faulkner-Walford, head chef

Radisson BLU Hotel, Frankland Lane, Durham, DH1 5TA,
Tel: 191 372 7200, www.radissonblu.co.uk/hotel-durham

LARGE MIXED ANTIPASTI

METHOD

For the Caponata: Sweat the onion and garlic in olive oil. Add the red wine vinegar and reduce. Add the tomatoes and aubergine. When soft, add the capers.

For the preserved tomatoes: Blanch the tomatoes and skin them. Place the tomatoes on a wire rack. Top with 2 thin slices of garlic, chopped thyme, good olive oil and the vincotto. Place in an oven for 1 to 2 hours at 65-70˚C until the tomatoes take on the appearance of juicy sundried tomatoes. Allow to cool and store in olive oil, use at will.

Putting it together: Blanch the green beans in salted water. Add the olive oil, chopped shallots and mint, then allow to cool naturally. Slice the meats and the salami, keep very thin at about .85 ml or ask your deli counter to cut for you. Fill the roasted pepper with basil pesto. Arrange on the plate as per photograph. Once arranged finish with a glug of good olive oil.

INGREDIENTS

Serves 1

4 slices Napoli salami
4 slices Milano salami
2 1/4 roasted peppers with pesto
3 slices rosemary ham
3 slices prosciutto di parma
50g green bean salad
75g caponata
4 tomatoes (marinated)
3 black olives
3 green olives

CAPONATA:

100 ml extra virgin olive oil
2 large aubergine
1tbs oregano (chopped)
1 red onion (diced)
50ml red wine vinegar
420g tomato (diced)
125g mixed olives (diced)
125g pine nuts (toasted)

PRESERVED TOMATOES :

Vine plum tomatoes
Fresh garlic
Olive oil
Thyme
Vincotto
Salt and pepper

GREEN BEANS:

500g green beans (topped and tailed)
5 tbs extra virgin olive oil
5 shallots (diced)
2 tsp mint (chopped)
Salt and pepper

Radisson BLU Hotel, Frankland Lane, Durham, DH1 5TA,
Tel: 191 372 7200, www.radissonblu.co.uk/hotel-durham

SPAGHETTI WITH CRAB MEAT & LIGHT SOAVE CREAM SAUCE

INGREDIENTS

Serves 1

- 100g spaghetti
- 50g crab meat
- 125ml mussel nage
- 30g tomato concasse
- 1 tbs butter
- 2 tbs chives (chopped)

NAGE:

- 4 tbs olive oil
- 2 kg mussels
- 3 carrots (diced)
- 3 shallots (diced)
- 1 fennel (diced)
- 2 cloves garlic (sliced)
- 1 celery stick (diced)
- 1 bay leaf
- 1 sprig thyme
- 1/2 bottle Soave white wine
- 1 litre double cream
- Salt and pepper

METHOD

For the nage: Soften the vegetables in the olive oil until they appear clear with no colour, remove from the pan. Heat the pan but do not burn, add the muscles and the wine then lid the pan and allow the muscles to steam, once all are open remove. Add the cream and reduce by 1/3.

For spaghetti of crab: Cook your spaghetti of choice (would recommend using high quality grade), drain. Add muscle nage to pan and reduce until rich. Toss cooked hot spaghetti in the pan with the nage, crab, chives and tomato concasse. Season with salt and pepper and serve. Finish with a little good olive oil.

Radisson BLU Hotel, Frankland Lane, Durham, DH1 5TA,
Tel: 191 372 7200, www.radissonblu.co.uk/hotel-durham

HONEY PANNA COTTA WITH LIME MARINATED BERRIES

INGREDIENTS

Serves 1

- 100g sugar
- 600ml double cream
- 150ml milk
- 4 tbs honey
- 6 cardamom pods
- 4 sheets gelatin
- 60 g berries
- 1 tbs sugar
- 1 tsp lime zest

METHOD

For the Panna Cotta: Line moulds with cling film and set aside. Soften the gelatin in cold water. Warm the cream, milk, honey and cardamom in a pan, and simmer gently for 10mins. Then add the soaked gelatin and stir until dissolved. Allow to infuse for a further 25mins. Strain the mix and pour in to lined moulds. Place in the fridge to set (should have the appearance of soft jelly when set).

For the berries: Cut the strawberries and place in a bowl with the rest of the fruit. Zest the lime and add to taste. Squeeze the lime and add to the rest of the mix, again to taste. Add the sugar until it equalizes the acidity of the lime juice. Stir the mix gently to release to juices of the berries.

To serve: Place the Panna Cotta on the desired plate. Spoon over the berries and juice. Garnish with a piece of fresh mint.

Radisson BLU Hotel, Frankland Lane, Durham, DH1 5TA,
Tel: 191 372 7200, www.radissonblu.co.uk/hotel-durham

THE RAT INN

THE RAT

THE RAT INN

Built around 1750 and situated in the picturesque hamlet of Anick,perched high above Hexham, the Rat Inn boasts spectacular views across the River Tyne and valley. Originally a drovers inn, for centuries there had been an alehouse in Anick,but just how the Rat came by what must surely be one of the oddest names for an Inn in Britain, remains shrouded in mystery, ask the locals and several interesting theories are offered! Perhaps the most intriguing tale tells of the then ale keeper who passed information to government spies during the Jacobite uprisings of the 18th century and thus became known as "the rat".

Phil and Karen took over the historic pub in late 2007,having previously owned the successful Green Room restaurant in Hexham. Taking care to retain the very special "pub" atmosphere which the Rat is famous for ,Phil has created a menu capturing classic British cooking, using seasonal ingredients, sourced locally. The menu is chalked on a board with dishes changing daily depending on what's available and fresh. A separate bar menu provides tasty sandwiches and lighter snacks, perfect with one of the six hand pulled ales on offer at the cosy bar.

With a stunning landscaped beer garden, exposed beams and roaring fires to sit by in winter, the Rat is a quintessential country Inn. Whatever its past, its been a welcoming and much loved village inn for well over 200 years, with visitors now travelling many miles to experience the delicious food and unique and very special atmosphere.

Anick, Hexham, Northumberland NE46 4LN
Tel: 01434 602814, www.theratinn.com

CUMBRIAN AIR DRIED HAM WITH CELERIAC AND APPLE REMOULADE

METHOD

If you find a great ingredient, there's no need to do too much to it. This air dried ham is produced by 7th and 8th generation family members from Richard Woodall's in Waberthwaite,Cumbria,using traditional time honoured methods. We often serve it simply with some pickles, homemade chutney and crusty brown bread. Alternatively, with this celeriac and apple remoulade it makes a deliciously simple cold starter, or light lunch, which can be prepared in advance.

Begin with the mayonnaise: Put the egg yolks,mustard,vinegar and seasoning in a bowl and whisk until smooth. Add the oil a few drops at a time and continue whisking until all the oil has been absorbed and the mixture is thick and creamy. This can be stored in the fridge for up to a few days. If you don't want to make your own, a good quality bought mayonnaise is fine.

For the remoulade: Cut the celeriac and apple into quarters, then peel and cut into as fine strips as you can manage. Mix immediately with the lemon juice and some sea salt, leave for around 30 mins. This will prevent the ingredients from turning brown, the salt will draw out some of the water giving the finished mix a more pliable texture and concentrated flavour. Add the mayonnaise, mustard and chopped parsley and mix.

To serve: Arrange the ham on the plate with the remoulade in the centre. Garnish with a sprig of parsley.

INGREDIENTS

Serves 4-6

1 packet of Woodalls air dried ham.

REMOULADE:

- 1 celeriac
- 2 Cox or granny Smith apples
- 4 tbs mayonnaise
- Juice of 1 lemon
- 1 tsp coarse grain mustard
- Chopped parsley (plus sprig to garnish)
- Sea salt and black pepper

MAYONNAISE:

- 2 egg yolks
- 2 tbs white wine vinegar
- 1 tbs Dijon mustard
- Salt and pepper
- 300ml groundnut oil

Anick, Hexham, Northumberland NE46 4LN
Tel: 01434 602814, www.theratinn.com

WEST MILL HILLS RACK OF LAMB WITH PROVENÇAL VEGETABLES, GARLIC AND ROSEMARY POTATOES, ROSEMARY JELLY

INGREDIENTS

Serves 2

1 six cutlet rack of lamb (ask your butcher to French trim it for you)
Olive oil to fry
Knob of butter
Garlic
6 roasting potatoes
1 bulb fennel
Rosemary sprigs
Sea salt and black pepper

PROVENCAL VEGETABLES:

1 red pepper (roughly chopped)
1 courgette (roughly chopped)
1 aubergine (roughly chopped)
1 red onion (roughly chopped)
1 yellow pepper (roughly chopped)
3 plum tomatoes (roughly chopped)

METHOD

We always have at least one dish "for two" on the menu; usually a Northumbria beef rib, we also include this dish when the new season's lamb is available and at its most tender and delicate.

To start: Heat oven to 200°C.

Provençal vegetables: fry onion in butter and a little olive oil until soft. Add courgette, pepper and aubergine, season and fry gently for a few minutes. Stir in tomatoes; to add an authentic Provencal flavour add a couple of pieces of dried orange peel to the mix(the zest of an orange is easily dried in a slow oven and keeps well in an airtight container as a great store cupboard ingredient). Cook for 30 mins until the sauce has reduced to a nice thick texture. Taste now; you may need to sweeten with a little sugar if the mix is bitter.

For the lamb: Season lamb with salt and pepper and seal meat side down in hot oil in a frying pan. Reduce the heat and cook on the fat side for a further couple of minutes until crispy. Transfer the pan to a hot oven(gas 6) and cook for 20 -25mins.Allow the meat to rest for around 15 mins before slicing.

To serve: Serve with some thinly sliced fennel fried in butter ,potatoes roasted with garlic and rosemary, Provençal vegetables and some Rosemary jelly.

Anick, Hexham, Northumberland NE46 4LN
Tel: 01434 602814, www.theratinn.com

THE RAT INN STEAK SARNIE

METHOD

The first dish we knew we had to have on our menu at the pub was a steak sandwich, we probably serve more steaks than anything else at the Rat so had to include one in this book. We use locally sourced beef rump for ours as we find it the tastiest, but you could use whichever cut you prefer, similarly you could substitute your favourite herbs in the marinade.

To start: Combine marinade ingredients, add the steak and leave to marinate in the fridge until needed, but for no more than 8 hours.

For the steak: Gently fry sliced onions in butter until soft, this can be done in advance then stored in the fridge until needed. Heat your frying pan until very, very hot, add the olive oil and fry the steak for a couple of minutes, then turn and cook for a further two minutes, depending on how you like yours cooked; we serve ours medium rare. Set the steak aside to rest. Add the onions to the pan to warm through. Meanwhile cut the bun in half and toast lightly. Place the steak on the lower half, cover with some of the onions and a Cos lettuce leaf. Drizzle some of the pan juices on the top half of the bun before closing.

To serve: Serve with thick cut chips and a pint of your favourite ale!

Note* Be prepared when cooking this, the smell will have them queueing up for more.

INGREDIENTS

Serves 1

6oz rump steak
Olive oil to fry
Cos lettuce
Sea salt and black pepper
1 onion (thinly sliced)
25g butter
1 crusty bun

MARINADE:

1 shallot (finely chopped)
Pinch of dried red chilli
2 tbs red wine
4 tbs olive oil
Clove of garlic
Ground black pepper
Herbs we use fresh from our garden usually a mix of, oregano, parsley, thyme (a pinch of each roughly chopped)

Anick, Hexham, Northumberland NE46 4LN
Tel: 01434 602814, www.theratinn.com

Seminary's peace set to be shattered

RIVERSIDE RESTAURANT

Bridge End, Barnard Castle, Co. Durham DL12 9BE, Tel: 01833 637 576, www.riverside-restaurant.co.uk

The people of Barnard Castle have been keeping a delightful secret to themselves for the past two years. But now, the secret is out; the Riverside Restaurant has been voted the "Best Small Restaurant in the North-East" at the Gourmet Society North East Restaurant Awards for 2009.

So what is it that has critics cooing and diners flocking to Andrew Rowbotham's venue? Quite simply, quality and imagination. Andrew promises "traditional British food with modern flair" for the diner. He said: "We use fresh, local, seasonal produce. Everything is made fresh to order - it is simple, it is fresh, it is honest food, that's what we're about. We're not reinventing, we're reviving slow cooked food."

Inside the restaurant there is a real sense of warmth enhanced by low beamed ceilings, an array of candles and Moorish scatter cushions. Service is relaxed and efficient, with friendly welcome and warm words to perfectly compliment your dinner. The sense of cosiness and comfy feel of the surroundings are made complete by a menu from heaven.

Founded on the principle of good food and service, the Riverside is all about quality. Starting with freshest, finest ingredients available locally and then turned with skill and passion into food to die for, the Riverside is truly a destination that wears its heart on its sleeve.

Andrew Rowbotham, owner

Bridge End, Barnard Castle, Co. Durham DL12 9BE
Tel: 01833 637 576, www.riverside-restaurant.co.uk

WARM SALAD OF WOOD PIGEON, BLACK PUDDING & RASPBERRY VINAIGRETTE

METHOD

To start: Season the pigeon breast with oil, sea salt and freshly ground pepper. Heat a heavy based frying pan until hot. Add the pigeon breasts skin side down and fry for about 1 - 2 minutes each side. They should feel slightly springy when pressed, transfer to a plate to rest cover them with foil to keep warm. Using the same pan as the pigeon, turn down the heat to medium, cut the black pudding into lengths season with salt and pepper, place them in the pan, cover with foil and cook on both sides for a couple of minutes until warmed through.

For the dressing: Combine the raspberries, vinegar and olive oil and blend until smooth. Place the salad leaves in a large bowl and drizzle with olive oil.

To serve: Arrange the salad onto serving plates. Slice the pigeon breast on an angle in half, arrange on top of the salad leaves, place 1 piece of black pudding per person and drizzle the raspberry vinaigrette as desired.

INGREDIENTS

Serves 4

4 skinless wood pigeon breasts

1 link or 200g good quality black pudding

Handful of fresh rocket leaves and fresh watercress

Groundnut or rapeseed oil

Sea salt and freshly ground black pepper (to season)

2 tbs extra virgin olive oil

DRESSING

55g raspberries

1 tbs raspberry vinegar

3 tbs rapeseed oil

1 tsp caster sugar

Bridge End, Barnard Castle, Co. Durham DL12 9BE
Tel: 01833 637 576, www.riverside-restaurant.co.uk

FILLET OF SEA BREAM, LEEKS, SCALLOPS & MUSSELS WITH LEMON & CHILLI BUTTER

INGREDIENTS

Serves 4

4 fresh fillets of sea bream
(400 / 600g whole fish)

12 fresh king scallops
(cleaned and coral removed)

12 large fresh mussels
(cleaned and de-bearded)

2 leeks
(trimmed and cut into long thin strips approx $^1/_2$ cm wide)

Sea salt and freshly ground black pepper

Splash of white wine

Groundnut or rapeseed oil (for frying)

25g butter

LEMON AND CHILLI BUTTER:

250g good quality butter

2 cloves fresh garlic
(peeled and crushed)

1 red chilli
(seeds removed and diced)

1 stalk of fresh lemongrass
(trim the bottom and remove outer leaves, chop coarsely)

1cm square of root ginger
(peeled and chopped)

Zest and juice of 1 lemon

2 tbs caster sugar

3 tbs groundnut
or rapeseed oil

METHOD

To start: Butter can be made in advance and stored for one week in the fridge or 3 months frozen. Cut butter into small cubes and put in bowl to soften. Warm oil gently, add chilli, ginger and lemon grass. Do not colour. Turn off heat and allow flavours to infuse. When cooled add lemon juice, zest and sugar and blend to a smooth paste. Pass paste through sieve then mix into butter. Lay out sheet of greaseproof paper and spoon butter into long sausage shape leaving 5cm at each end. Roll butter into cylinder shape ensuring no air pockets. Twist ends and refrigerate for at least 2 hrs.

To prepare: Heat a large sauce pan, pour in white wine allow to boil, once boiling add mussels, replace lid, cook until all mussels have opened. Set aside the cooked mussels, keep warm and strain cooking liquor from pan, reserve to use later. Gently score the skin of each fish fillet, this stops them curling up as they cook. Put a non-stick frying pan over a medium-high heat and add the oil. Lightly season the fillets and place skin-side down in the oil for 2 -3 minutes, place in the oven on a non-stick tray for 2 minutes or until the flesh is no longer opaque. Heat a medium sauce pan, add the reserved cooking liquor from the mussels, reduce by half, add the butter followed by leek strips and the cooked mussels, cook for 1-2 minutes until leeks have turned opaque. Turn off heat and set aside. Heat a frying pan to full heat, drizzle the hot pan with oil, lightly season the scallops and arrange in a clockwise rotation around the pan. Once all of the scallops are in the pan, turn them all over beginning with the first one and follow your clockwise rotation. Lay out 4 bowls, arrange the leek strips in the centre, alternate 3 scallops and 3 mussels around the bowl, spoon some of the cooking liquor from the leek and mussels over the leeks and set the fish fillet skin side up on top of the leeks. Cut 3 disks from the lemon and chilli butter and sit on the top of the scallops.

Bridge End, Barnard Castle, Co. Durham DL12 9BE
Tel: 01833 637 576, www.riverside-restaurant.co.uk

RHUBARB & CUSTARD WITH RHUBARB SPRING ROLLS

RIVERSIDE RESTAURANT

INGREDIENTS

Serves 4

- 150ml milk
- 100 ml double cream
- 25g sugar
- 4 egg yolks
- ½ vanilla pod or ½ tsp essence
- 800g forced rhubarb (trimmed)
- 150g caster sugar
- 4 sheets filo pastry
- 50g butter (melted)
- Caster sugar (for sprinkling)

METHOD

To start: Cover the Rhubarb in the sugar, leave overnight in the fridge. Heat the milk and cream in a heavy bottomed pan, add the vanilla, in another bowl mix egg yolks and sugar until smooth, once the milk mixture has boiled sieve into a jug then mix the hot liquid continuously into the egg mixture until combined. Sieve the liquid once again to remove any egg strands. Pour the finished custard into 5cm oven proof ramekins. Place in a roasting tin, pour in boiling water until half of the outside of the ramekin is covered, bake for 30 – 35mins 160°C. After 30mins gently shake from side to side, if the custard is set with a slight wobble in the very centre remove and chill, if not leave for 5 mins and repeat. Heat a wide heavy bottomed pan to medium heat, strain liquid from rhubarb and add the liquid to the pan. Bring to the boil and reduce by half, once your liquid has reduced add the rhubarb pieces and stir for a couple of minutes until tender. Remove from the liquid with a slotted spoon, set aside. Once cool separate the cooked rhubarb into two bowls. Set aside the reduced rhubarb syrup.

For the puree: Take 2/3's of the remaining bowl of rhubarb, blend and add the reduced rhubarb syrup until it reaches a nice thick syrup.

For the Spring rolls: Take a bowl of rhubarb and strain until as dry as possible. Cut the pastry into squares approx 15 x 15cms. Brush one sheet with butter and lay a second sheet on top. Place a line of the cooked rhubarb mixture in a horizontal line 2 cms from the top. Roll over and turn the edges in, brushing with butter and roll into a cigar shape. Use immediately. Deep fry at 180°C until golden brown, sprinkle with caster sugar.

To serve: To serve take the chilled custard pot, use the remaining 1/3 of a bowl of rhubarb to garnish, top with a little of the syrup. Arrange the Rhubarb and Custard pot, spring roll and rhubarb puree on the plate.

Bridge End, Barnard Castle, Co. Durham DL12 9BE
Tel: 01833 637 576, www.riverside-restaurant.co.uk

SACHINS

Forth Banks, Newcastle upon Tyne NE1 3SG, Tel: 0191 232 4660 / 261 9035, www.sachins.co.uk

"At Sachins we pride ourselves in being a unique Punjabi restaurant, offering the finest in Indian cuisine on Newcastle's Quayside. Just as I fell in love with Newcastle, the architecture and location of the restaurant seemed ideal when I first visited. My great passion for Indian cuisine and the expert skills gained during my years at the hands of Executive Chef, Dinesh Rawlley has all helped form the foundations for an exquisite restaurant.

"The delicate use of spices and distinctive cooking methods of the tandoor creates a wonderful dining experience for any individual. Our unique menu has seen us win praise from critics and customers alike. Our flavours don't overpower the less mature palette, so we are perfect for those unfamiliar with Punjabi cuisine. We provide our loyal customers with exclusive, creative dishes made with only the freshest and finest ingredients to truly demonstrate the art of eating well.

"The setting of the restaurant on Forth Banks provides an accessible location for those in the city and on the riverside. The contemporary, chic style creates a relaxing atmosphere to spend an evening and taste the exotic flavours. At Sachins we can accommodate for a variety of occasions, from weddings and birthdays to business meals and conferences. Throughout our 27 years in Newcastle, Sachins has earned a first class reputation and attracts visitors from all over the region with our speciality dishes and unique flavours.
Sachins – The finest Punjabi Cuisine – The Art of Eating Well – Punjabi Style.

Bob Arora, chef and owner

Forth Banks, Newcastle upon Tyne NE1 3SG
Tel: 0191 232 4660 / 261 9035, www.sachins.co.uk

FISH TIKKA

METHOD

To start: Wash and dry the cubed fish fillets. Sprinkle salt and lemon juice. Set aside to marinate for half an hour. Add yoghurt to a bowl and mix with the remaining ingredients and whisk well. Pour mixture over pieces of fish and coat evenly. Leave to marinate for at least one hour.

To cook: Pre heat oven to 175 °C. Place fish on baking tray. Cook until golden brown and thoroughly cooked.

INGREDIENTS

Serves 2

- Cut fish into equal size cubes
- Salt to taste
- 15ml lemon juice
- 120g yoghurt
- 15ml vinegar (sirka)
- 15g Garam Masala
- 10g ground cumin seeds (Jeera)
- 10g ajwain seeds
- 10g red chilli powder
- 10g garlic paste
- Oil or butter (for basting)

Forth Banks, Newcastle upon Tyne NE1 3SG
Tel: 0191 232 4660 / 261 9035, www.sachins.co.uk

MURGH (CHICKEN) MUGLAI

INGREDIENTS

Serves 2

- 175ml natural yoghurt
- 2 tsp turmeric
- 1 clove garlic
- 1.5 kg chicken (cut into equal size pieces)
- 125g vegetable oil
- 2 large onions (sliced)
- 1 tsp of ground ginger
- 2" piece of cinnamon stick
- 5 cloves (Laung)
- 5 ground cardamom pods
- 1 tbs crushed coriander seeds
- 1 tsp ground cumin
- 1/2 tsp chilli powder
- 1 tsp salt
- 2 tsp almond flakes (to garnish)
- Coriander leaves (to garnish)

METHOD

To start: Put the yoghurt, turmeric and a clove of garlic into a food processor and blend to a smooth paste.

For the chicken: Put the chicken pieces into a dish and pour the mixture over the chicken. Cover the dish and leave to marinate in the fridge overnight. Get a non stick pan and add the oil and warm through. Once the oil has warmed, add finely chopped onions and keep stirring until caramelised. Add remaining spices and continually keep stirring. Add chicken pieces with any remaining yoghurt marinade. Cover the pan with a tight fitting lid and simmer for about 45 minutes stirring occasionally (add water if you like the dish to have more sauce).

To serve: Once the chicken has cooked through, transfer to a serving dish and scatter with almond flakes and coriander.

Forth Banks, Newcastle upon Tyne NE1 3SG
Tel: 0191 232 4660 / 261 9035, www.sachins.co.uk

SACHINS

KHEER (INDIAN RICE PUDDING)

METHOD

To start: Place rice and 1½ pints of milk in a heavy bottomed pan. Cook gently at simmering point for 45 - 60 minutes until most of the milk has been absorbed. Add the remaining milk and sultanas and stir well and continue simmering until thickened. Remove from the heat and add sugar to taste. Leave until completely cold, stirring occasionally to prevent a skin forming and then add the cream.

To serve: Place Kheer into small dishes and add almond flakes and pistachio nuts for decoration.

INGREDIENTS

Serves 2

- 75g long grain rice
- 3 pints of milk
- 50g sultanas
- Caster sugar (to taste)
- 50ml single cream
- Flaked almonds and pistachios (for decoration)

Forth Banks, Newcastle upon Tyne NE1 3SG
Tel: 0191 232 4660 / 261 9035, www.sachins.co.uk

SIX RESTAURANT AT BALTIC

BALTIC Centre for Contemporary Art, South Shore Road, Gateshead NE8 3BA Tel: 0191 440 4948, www.sixbaltic.com

BALTIC FLOUR M

SIX is the stunning rooftop restaurant at BALTIC Centre for Contemporary Art combining breathtaking panoramic views of the River Tyne with great food, great service and a great experience.

Named due to its location on the gallery's sixth floor, when it comes to restaurants with similar views the only comparison to SIX to come anywhere close would be the OXO Tower in London or Harvey Nichols in Edinburgh.

Brought to you by Fresh Element, Executive Chef Richard Sim prepares his trademark style of food, best described as British modern cuisine featuring the very best ingredients, simply cooked and served in a relaxed and friendly setting.

Former Executive Chef of the prestigious Alnwick Garden Treehouse Restaurant, Richard has over 20 years experience in working at some of the country's most coveted restaurants, and was awarded the accolade of North East Chef of the Year. He specialises in producing dishes of exceptional quality using ingredients sourced from the region's finest artisan producers.

Fish from North Shields, Ingram Valley lamb, slow-cooked Northumbrian duck leg, Blagdon pork, Boulmer crab cakes and comfort puddings like jam roly poly are all on the menu, which boasts a wide range of dishes including popular favourites such as pan fried supreme of Northumbrian duck with elderflower and roast garlic and carpaccio of locally caught cod with warm horseradish potato salad.

Chefs from SIX

BALTIC Centre for Contemporary Art, South Shore Road, Gateshead NE8 3BA Tel: 0191 440 4948, www.sixbaltic.com

CHILLI SALT FRIED SQUID WITH ASIAN DIPPING SAUCE

METHOD

For the dipping sauce: Mix all of the dipping sauce ingredients together and stir well.

For the squid: Soak the squid in the milk. Mix together the corn flour, salt, chilli and breadcrumbs in a bowl. Pass the squid through the breadcrumb mixture, shake off any excess and place in very hot oil (eg a deep fat fryer as hot as it goes) for no more than 1 minute. Only fry a small amount at a time. Drain on paper.

To serve: Serve with the dipping sauce.

INGREDIENTS

Serves 4

- 1lb fresh squid (cleaned and scored)
- 100ml milk (for soaking squid)
- 55g Maldon sea salt (or salt flakes)
- 110g corn flour
- 55g Japanese breadcrumbs
- 15g chilli flakes (add more if you like it hot!)

ASIAN DIPPING SAUCE

- 60ml plum sauce
- 60ml hoi sin sauce
- 60ml soy sauce
- 60ml sweet chilli sauce
- 60ml mango chutney
- 55g toasted sesame seeds

BALTIC Centre for Contemporary Art, South Shore Road, Gateshead NE8 3BA Tel: 0191 440 4948, www.sixbaltic.com

SILVER DARLINGS WITH SALAD NICOISE

INGREDIENTS	METHOD

Serves 4

8 fresh sardines
4 slices of sourdough bread

SALAD NICOISE

85g green beans (trimmed and blanched)
85g small Jersey royal potatoes (just cooked then halved)
55g good black olives
35g capers
2 sun blushed tomatoes
4 free range eggs (boiled for 6 minutes then quartered)
4 anchovy fillets
Mixed salad leaves
Extra virgin olive oil (for salad dressing)
Balsamic vinegar (for salad dressing)
Salt and pepper (for seasoning)

CARROT SALSA

4 large carrots (peeled and sliced thinly)
1 bulb of fennel (sliced thinly)
2 large shallots (finely chopped)
30g fennel seeds
90ml white wine vinegar
55g caster sugar

METHOD

For the carrot salsa: Boil the vinegar, sugar and fennel seeds. Add the sliced carrot, shallot and fennel. Remove from heat and leave to cool.

For the sardines: Season the sardines and place under a hot grill for 2-3 minutes each side. Toast the sourdough bread.

For the salad nicoise: Combine the green beans, potatoes, olives, capers, tomatoes, eggs, anchovies and salad leaves. Dress with the oil and balsamic vinegar.

To serve: Place a slice of the toasted bread on a plate, spoon on the carrot salsa and lay the sardines on top. Serve with the salad.

BALTIC Centre for Contemporary Art, South Shore Road, Gateshead NE8 3BA Tel: 0191 440 4948, www.sixbaltic.com

BAILEYS COFFEE AND CRISPY DOUGHNUTS

METHOD

For the chocolate mousse: Melt the chocolate in a bowl over a pan of hot water. Fold in the egg yolks, cream, egg whites and sugar. Spoon into the bottom of a latte glass and place in the fridge to set.

For the Baileys mousse: Melt the gelatine into the espresso, then whisk in the Baileys and cream. Fold in the egg whites and sugar. Layer on top of the chocolate mousse and leave to set.

For the doughnuts: Crumble ½ oz fresh yeast into the water then mix in the flour and allow to ferment for 20 minutes. Crumble the other ½ oz fresh yeast into the milk then mix in the flour followed by the sugar, egg yolks and butter. Add the ferment mixture then mix for 6 minutes or until you have a soft dough which is not too wet or dry. Cut out the doughnuts using a ring cutter. Provė for 15 minutes. Deep fry for 1 minute on each side or until golden brown.

To serve: Spoon the whipped condensed milk onto the top of the mousse and serve with the doughnuts.

INGREDIENTS

Serves 4

CHOCOLATE MOUSSE

110g dark chocolate
55g sugar
120ml cream (whipped)
2 egg yolks
2 egg whites
(whisked until light and fluffy)

BAILEYS MOUSSE

235ml cream (whipped)
2 shots of espresso (hot)
50ml Baileys
2 egg whites
(whisked until light and fluffy)
3 leaves of gelatine
55g sugar

TOPPING

355ml condensed milk
(whipped until fluffy)

DOUGHNUTS

Ferment:
30ml water
15g fresh yeast
110g flour

Dough:
15g fresh yeast
28ml milk
225g flour
40g sugar
2 egg yolks
30g butter

BALTIC Centre for Contemporary Art, South Shore Road, Gateshead NE8 3BA Tel: 0191 440 4948, www.sixbaltic.com

THE STABLES

Here at The Stables we are passionate about food and aim to give our customers a fine dining experience in a relaxed atmosphere at affordable prices every time. Our emphasis is on quality locally-sourced fresh ingredients to deliver a wide-ranging menu which appeals to all tastes - something for everyone.

Judging by the comments we receive and the repeat business we enjoy, we are succeeding in serving top quality food to our regulars from the Wynyard estate as well as visitors from further afield. Food critics have been highly complementary of our friendly staff, great service, how extensive and varied our menu is and most importantly of all about the quality of our food. For example the Sunday Sun's hard-to-please Eddy Eats gave us top marks and a glowing reference for our Sunday lunches.

We also listen to customers and have now made the full menu available for take away since we have had so many requests.We are open every lunchtime serving food from 12 till 2.30pm Monday to Saturday then in the evenings from 5.30 to 9pm. On Sunday food is served until 5pm.

My partner Julie and I are very proud of our reputation for great food. We look forward to warmly welcoming you very soon.

Marc Everson, chef proprietor

The Granary, Wynyard Village TS22 5QQ
Tel: 01740 644 074

SWEET POTATO AND ROASTED DUCK SOUP

METHOD

To start: Place the sweet potatoes on a well oiled roasting tray and place in the oven on a medium heat until cooked. While the potatoes are in the oven put the water into a sauce pan with the fresh grated ginger and bring to the boil. When the potatoes are cooked let them cool down enough for you to peel the skins off then chop the flesh and return it to the pan and bring back to the boil. With a hand blender blitz the soup until smooth. Season to taste. In a frying pan cook the duck and other ingredients until nicely browned.

To serve: Serve in a bowl with duck mixture on top.

INGREDIENTS

Serves 4

- 3 large sweet potatoes
- 1" long piece of ginger
- Aromatic duck
- 1 whole chillie deseeded
- Handful of coriander
- Handful of mint
- 1 tsp of lime zest
- 1 tbs of fish sauce
- Juice of 1 lime
- 1 litre of water

The Granary, Wynyard Village TS22 5QQ
Tel: 01740 644 074

PAN ROASTED COD WITH NEW POTATOES, CHORIZO, ROCKET & SUNBLUSHED TOMATOES AND BALSAMIC

INGREDIENTS

Serves 2

- 6oz cod fillet
- 5 cooked new potatoes
- 100g chorizo
- Bunch of rocket
- 40g sunblushed tomatoes
- Aged balsamic vinegar

METHOD

To start: Pan fry cod until nicely coloured and finish off in the oven until cooked. In another frying pan start frying the new potatoes in olive oil until browned then add chorizo and grill for one minute. Add the sunblushed tomatoes and return to grill for a further 20 seconds.

To serve: Place the mixture in the centre of a large bowl or plate, place the rocket on next, then the cod and drizzle some balsamic vinegar around the plate.

The Granary, Wynyard Village TS22 5QQ
Tel: 01740 644 074

ICED HAZELNUT NOUGAT

METHOD

To make the praline: Heat 100g of sugar in a pan until it turns a caramel colour then stir in the hazelnuts. Pour onto a cooled oiled tray and when cold break into pieces. In a bowl, whisk the egg whites then whisk in the remaining amount of sugar to make a stiff meringue. In another bowl whisk the cream until stiff then fold the whipped cream into the meringue then add the praline mixture and pour into moulds and put in the freezer until set hard.

To serve: Take the moulds from the freezer, heat the sides with a blow torch carefully for 2 seconds, place on a plate and decorate with strawberries.

INGREDIENTS

Serves 6

- 4 egg whites
- 400ml double cream
- 400g caster sugar
- Handful of shelled hazelnuts

The Granary, Wynyard Village TS22 5QQ
Tel: 01740 644 074

STARTERS & PUDS

BCA
CROSBYS

To look at the entrance to Starters & Puds gives little clue as to just how extensive the restaurant actually is once you walk down the stairs into the space below.

The restaurant is located in the vaults of an old bank in Shakespeare Street in the heart of Grainger Town in Newcastle. Step down from the street and you enter an amazing world of barrel-vaulted ceilings, open brickwork and intriguing rooms, each with its own atmosphere.

We believe at Starters & Puds to source good quality ingredients which are mainly purchased locally. The use of fresh and organic produce is prevalent throughout the menu and we cater for many dietary requirements including vegetarian and gluten free.

The location of Starters & Puds beside the Theatre Royal means that we are very popular with theatre goers. Because we are open all day pre theatre diners can arrive when they want and have plenty of time to have something to eat before the performance – and because we are only twenty yards away you have plenty of time to stroll across the road. If you want to make the evening ,more of an occasion we are happy to serve starters and that bottle of wine pre theatre, take your order for puds and serve those and your wine back on your table after the performance, perhaps returning and making use of those leather chesterfields?

David Burrow

2-6 Shakespeare Street, Newcastle Upon Tyne NE1 6AQ
Tel:0191 233 2515, www.startersandpuds.co.uk

STARTERS & PUDS

SEARED SCALLOPS WITH CAULIFLOWER PUREE, BEETROOT PUREE, RUM SOAKED RAISINS & SHISO LEAVES

METHOD

For the raisins: Place the rum and raisins in a bowl (ideally the day before) and allow the alcohol to soak into the raisins.

For the cauliflower puree: Break the cauliflower into florets and put in a pan of boiling, salted water with the juice of 1 lemon, and cook until soft. Place in a food processor and blend with the double cream until smooth. Season to taste and put through a fine sieve to ensure no lumps.

For the beetroot puree: Place the cooked beetroot into a food processor and blend (you may need a touch of water to make a smooth puree). Check seasoning then put through a fine sieve as before.

For the scallops: Cook the scallops in a medium hot pan with a touch of oil and butter. Cook on all sides until cooked.

To serve: Place the cauliflower puree into a piping bag and pipe three small piles. Then quenelle three small pieces of beetroot puree. Place the scallops on the plate and sprinkle over the raisins. Finish with the shiso leaves.

INGREDIENTS

Serves 4

12 scallops

1/2 cauliflower

1 lemon

50ml double cream

1/2 packet cooked beetroot

50g raisins

50ml dark rum

100g shiso leaves
or micro herbs

2-6 Shakespeare Street, Newcastle Upon Tyne NE1 6AQ
Tel:0191 233 2515, www.startersandpuds.co.uk

PAN ROASTED NORTHUMBERLAND VENISON, PARSNIP PUREE, WHOLE ROASTED WILD MUSHROOMS, RICH RED WINE JUS AND PARSNIP CRISPS

INGREDIENTS

Serves 4

- 4 x 150g venison loins (steaks will do)
- 200g parsnips
- 120g wild mushrooms
- 100ml milk
- 2kg venison bones (beef will do)
- 1 large onion
- 2 large carrots
- 3 cloves garlic
- 1 leek
- 1 head celery
- 2 bottles of good red wine
- 50g tomato puree
- Olive oil (for cooking)

METHOD

For the stock: This should be done at least the day before but two days before is best. Place bones in roasting tin with tomato puree smeared on top, bake in hot oven until golden. Roughly cut onion, carrots, garlic, leek and celery. Heat a large heavy based pan with a little oil then when smoking add vegetables stirring until browned. Add a bottle of red wine, remove any brown bits from bottom of pan and reduce by two thirds. Remove browned bones from tray and place into pan and top with COLD water. Bring to the boil reduce heat, simmer for about 8 hours, skim any residue that rises to the top. Remove from pan and sieve into container, refrigerate overnight and remove excess cold fat in the morning. Heat a saucepan and add the other bottle of red wine, reduce by half then add the cold stock bring to boil and reduce until sauce consistency is achieved.

For the parsnips: Peel parsnips, leaving 12 nice slices for deep frying later for crisps. Roughly chop the rest, put in saucepan with milk and top with water. Once parsnip is cooked remove liquid from pan and place in a food processor check the seasoning and sieve. Cook the parsnip crisps in deep fat fryer.

To cook: Clean the mushrooms and allow to air dry on a tea towel. Heat a frying pan with a little oil and butter then place in the well seasoned venison seal on all sides and place in oven until cooked. Once s cooked remove from heat and allow to rest. Heat another frying pan with oil and butter, fry the now dry mushrooms again making sure well seasoned.

To serve: Place a line of puree down the middle of the plate. Slice the venison and place the opposite way. Place the mushrooms around. Drizzle over the sauce and top with parsnip crisps.

2-6 Shakespeare Street, Newcastle Upon Tyne NE1 6AQ
Tel:0191 233 2515, www.startersandpuds.co.uk

ASSIETTE OF RASPBERRIES RASPBERRY FRANGIPANE, MOUSSE, BRULEE, JELLY & COULIS

METHOD

For the pastry: Rub flour and butter together until mixture resembles coarse breadcrumbs. Add sugar, lemon zest and pinch of salt. Work in egg yolk and vanilla extract until forms smooth dough. Roll into ball, wrap in cling film, chill for at least 1 hour (or up to 2 days).

For frangipane (almond cream): Mix all ingredients until well combined. (This will keep in the fridge for up to 4 days.) Roll out the chilled pastry to the thickness of a £1 coin, line a 25cm loose-bottomed tart tin. Trim the pastry. Chill or freeze tart case for at least 1 hour. Place frangipane mixture in pastry case top with raspberries and put in pre heated oven 200˚C and bake for 30-40 minutes. Trim off overhanging pastry with a small knife. Remove from tin and leave to cool on a wire rack. In a saucepan combine 350g raspberries and sugar. Stir in gelatin. Remove from heat and scrape into a large bowl. Cool for 5 mins. Remove chilled whipped cream from refrigerator. Mix 250g of whipped cream into raspberry mixture until well combined. Fold in remaining whipped cream. Pour into wine glasses and chill. Pre heat the oven to 140˚C. In a medium bowl whisk the sugar and eggs together.

To prepare: Divide raspberries between 4 x 1 cup ramekin dishes. Heat milk and cream along with the scraped vanilla bean. Transfer to the egg mixture, mix and pour into the ramekins. Place in a bain-marie of hot water and bake in the oven for 40 minutes. Allow to cool and set, then chill in the fridge. Sprinkle the tops with caster sugar and glaze under a hot grill until golden. Soak gelatin leaf in cold water until pliable.

For the coulis: Place all ingredients in a saucepan and boil. Seive, keeping 250ml of liquid. Add gelatin leaf, place in moulds. Liquidise remaining liquid and seive to make the coulis.

To serve: Place various components on plate in nice pattern and drizzle a little of the coulis over.

INGREDIENTS

Serves 4

FRANGIPANE:
- 200g plain flour
- 140g unsalted butter, (cut into small pieces)
- 100g golden caster sugar
- Zest of 1 lemon (finely grated)
- 1 egg yolk
- A few drops of vanilla extract
- 85g unsalted butter (room temperature)
- 85g golden caster sugar
- 85g ground almonds
- 1 egg

MOUSSE:
- 500g fresh raspberries
- 1 tbs unflavored gelatin
- 1 tbs lemon juice
- 1 litre whipped cream
- 60g caster sugar

BRULEE:
- 75g caster sugar
- 5 egg yolks
- 100g raspberries (frozen if fresh unavailable)
- 50 ml milk
- 450 ml double cream
- 1 vanilla pod

COULIS AND JELLY:
- 200g raspberries
- 50g caster sugar
- 200ml water
- 1 gelatine leaf

2-6 Shakespeare Street, Newcastle Upon Tyne NE1 6AQ
Tel:0191 233 2515, www.startersandpuds.co.uk

THE WAITING ROOM

9 Station Rd, Eaglescliffe, Stockton-On-Tees, Cleveland TS16 0BU, Tel: 01642 780465, www.the-waiting-room.co.uk

Puddings £4.95
• Raspberry & Coconut Tarte
• Spiced apple Crumble
• Icecream & Butterscotch Sauce
• Sticky Toffee Pudding
• Marmalade Bread & Butter Pud
• Lemon cheesecake
also we have strawberry
or raspberry Sam Smiths beer

THE WAITING ROOM

Photograph Robert Paige

The Waiting Room was voted amongst the top 40 restaurants in the UK in the Observer Newspaper food awards for 2008, and in 2009 the homely hideaway was named Best Restaurant in The UK by The Vegetarian Society, whilst The BBC commented that it is a "wonderful restaurant, selling great food".

The Waiting Room is a charming, popular restaurant where lovely wholesome dishes have been created for 25 years. Recipes are developed with every change of season; beautifully rustic meals are served up with bold simplicity and full of big natural flavours. The excellent menu, which changes with each season is complemented with a great list of organic and wines and beers, and a daily blackboard of gorgeous homemade puddings.

Sunday evenings bring a change of format, when some incredible musicians and performers play in a back room cabaret setting, with a tailored menu.

The Waiting Room will have been established for 25 years in 2010, and to celebrate this anniversary work is underway on an eagerly anticipated book of the restaurant and it's famous food. Customers can register their interest in the book on the restaurant's excellent website.

Images courtesy of Gilmar Ribeiro

Luke Harding, proprietor

9 Station Rd, Eaglescliffe, Stockton-On-Tees, Cleveland TS16 0BU
Tel: 01642 780465, www.the-waiting-room.co.uk

TIKKA HALLAUBERLOUMI

METHOD

For the aubergine: Slice the aubergine into 7mm discs. Salt and stand for 45 minutes. Rinse off salt and pat dry. Marinate the aubergine in a tikka paste for a minimum of 20 minutes. Roast the marinated aubergine on a tray and greased baking sheet for in a moderately hot oven for 15 mins or so until just starting to brown.

For the halloumi: Make 7mm slices of the halloumi, dust with a tikka powder mix. Fry the dusted halloumi in a griddle pan until softened and coloured. Pair each slice of halloumi with a slice of aubergine, Mix a tea spoon of tikka powder with yoghurt. Drizzle the tikka yoghurt mix, over each aubergine and halloumi slice and glaze beneath grill.

To make Tikka paste powder: Tikka is a blend of groundspices; coriander, cumin, paprika, tumeric, chilli ginger garlic and garam masala. A good smoked paprika adds a nice dusky flavour to the blend.

INGREDIENTS

Serves 3

- 1 large aubergine
- 125g block of halloumi
- Tikka powdered spice mix
- Ground nut oil
- Natural yoghurt

9 Station Rd, Eaglescliffe, Stockton-On-Tees, Cleveland TS16 0BU
Tel: 01642 780465, www.the-waiting-room.co.uk

ASPARAGUS AND HAZELNUT ROULADE

INGREDIENTS

Serves 3

- 14 eggs
- 4 asparagus bunches (Trim woody ends)
- 225g hazelnuts
- 225g béchamel sauce
- Splash of double cream
- 55g self raising flour

PEA PUREE:

- 300g garden peas
- 300ml crème freche

METHOD

Separate eggs: Add a pinch of salt to the egg whites and beat them to a soft peak. Add what is left on the end of the whisk of the foamed whites to the yolks, and beat the yolks, whilst adding the self raising flour until they become pale and fluffy. Gently fold the beaten whites and yolks together with a touch of pepper seasoning. Line an 18 inch shallow tray with parchment and pour in the egg mix. Place in a moderate pre-heated oven 180-190˚C for 25 mins, until colouring.

Blanch the asparagus, until tender and refresh immediately in cold running water. Trim off the pretty tips – the top 3-4 inches. Roughly chop the remainder and stir this rough chopped asparagus in with the cooled béchamel sauce with the chopped hazelnuts. Place the cool baked egg soufflé shell onto a fresh piece of baking parchment. Spread the filling generously over the roulade shell. Retain half of the tips for garnish and space out the other half across the filling of the roulade. Now lifting the edge of the parchment, roll the shell gently across its length, creating an 18inch long roulade.

For the pea puree: Slacken the crème freche with a splash of single cream. Blitz the peas and crème fresh, seasoning with salt pepper and optional lemon and mint.

To serve: Slice and warm gently, decorate.

9 Station Rd, Eaglescliffe, Stockton-On-Tees, Cleveland TS16 0BU
Tel: 01642 780465, www.the-waiting-room.co.uk

MARMALADE BRIOCHE BREAD AND BUTTER PUD

METHOD

To start: Slice buns in half, and layer within buttered baking dish, spreading each layer (3 in total) with butter and marmalade.

For custard mix: Whisk up the eggs, cream and sugar into a custardy mix pour this mix over the brioche within the baking tray leave to soak for 30 mins (cover with cling film and weigh down with a plate)

Finally: Remove cling film, place in 160°C oven until the bake is set but wobbly.

INGREDIENTS

Serves 1

- 24 brioche buns
- A jar of good marmalade (homemade)
- 115g butter
- 6 eggs and 2 yolks
- 115g sugar
- 250ml milk
- 250ml cream

9 Station Rd, Eaglescliffe, Stockton-On-Tees, Cleveland TS16 0BU
Tel: 01642 780465, www.the-waiting-room.co.uk

WAREN HOUSE HOTEL

Bamburgh, Northumberland NE70 7EE, Tel: 01668 214581, www.warenhousehotel.co.uk

The Waren House
Hotel
Steve Owens

I started working in the kitchen as a pot washer at the age of 13 years and worked my way up through the ranks till I became head chef at the grand old age of 18. My training, mostly self taught, has never taken me out of Northumberland and now 22 years on I am the head chef at the Waren House Hotel and have been for the last 4 years. The Waren House, owned by Peter and Anita Laverack, is majestically placed on the North Eastern coastline just outside Bamburgh at Budle Bay. Our location offers today's visitor a rare retreat for true relaxation, along with a central point for venturing through the delights of North Northumberland and the Scottish Borders.

At the Waren House our food can be described as classical cookery with a modern Northumbrian twist, and using locally sauced ingredients we not only provide our diners with a taste of Northumberland but also support our local producers and suppliers. Our menu changes daily. Stocks, sorbets, soups, sweets, petits fours, breads and accompaniments are made in house which can be challenging for my team of three chefs and i but also very rewarding. The front of house staff help make for the perfect experience with their friendly welcome, smiling faces and 'nothing too much' attitude. I'm very proud of the whole team and the mutual respect, shown to customers and colleagues alike, make the Waren House a great place to work and a 'home from home' experience for our guests.

Steven Owens, head chef

Bamburgh, Northumberland NE70 7EE
Tel: 01668 214581, www.warenhousehotel.co.uk

WAREN HOUSE HOTEL

CRASTER SMOKED SALMON, ROCKET AND RICOTTA TORTELLINI, CITRUS TARTER AND TEMPURA TARTLET WITH HOLLANDAISE AND ROCKET OIL

METHOD

For the tortellini: Place the flour in a food processor with rocket and blend, add the egg and season, blend to a firm ball but not sticky Pass through a pasta machine to the thinnest setting and cut to discs with a scone cutter. Dice up the smoked salmon and bind with the ricotta cheese, season then add to the centre of each disc and shape. Cook in boiling salted water with a touch of oil for 3 minutes.

For the citrus tarter: Dice up the smoked salmon and add the herbs to taste. Just before serving, bind with some of the dressing (too early and the tarter will cook from the citrus in the dressing).

For the tempura tartlets: Mix all the batter ingredients in a processor. Heat some oil in a deep pan. Submerge a metal ladle until hot, remove the ladle and dip the base into the batter mixture, this will immediately start to cook. Tap the ladle and the basket will fall. Cook in the oil until crisp and dry on kitchen paper.

For the hollandaise: Blend the egg yolks with the dressing, slowly add warm butter until a 'whipped cream' consistency is reached.

For the rocket oil: Blend the oil and rocket together, season and strain.

To serve: Place a cooked tortellini on the plate and press some tarter into a mould and tip out. Place a tempura basket on the plate, add the smoked salmon and hollandaise, and serve with a drizzle of citrus dressing and rocket oil.

INGREDIENTS

Serves 4

TORTELLINI:

75g smoked salmon
75g ricotta cheese
140g pasta flour
Pinch salt
1 egg
1 egg yolk
Plunch of rocket

CITRUS TARTER:

100g smoked salmon
Chopped fresh parsley, dill and chives

CITRUS DRESSING:

1 small cup of mixed citrus juice
3 small cups of oliefera oil
½ tsp of Dijon mustard
Pinch of castor sugar
Pinch of salt
(all blended in a processor)

TEMPURA TARTLET:

Smoked salmon
50g self-raising flour
1 small egg yolk
½ tsp cornflour
75ml ice cold water
2 egg whites

HOLLANDAISE SAUCE:

2 egg yolks
1tbs citrus dressing (above)
125g butter

ROCKET OIL:

Plunch of rocket
1 cup oleifera oil
Seasoning

Bamburgh, Northumberland NE70 7EE
Tel: 01668 214581, www.warenhousehotel.co.uk

PIPERFIELD PORK NOISETTES WITH COMFIT OF SHOULDER, CREAMED BLACK PUDDING, VEGETABLE TERRINE, PANCETTA, HERITAGE POTATO MUSTARD MASH AND APPLE CHUTNEY JUS

INGREDIENTS

Serves 4

PORK NOISETTES:

2 tenderloin pork noisettes

COMFIT OF SHOULDER:

Shoulder of pork
1 chopped carrot,
onion and 1/2 a leek
Goose fat
Sprig of thyme
Slices of cured ham

CREAMED BLACK PUDDING:

250g black pudding
100ml cream

VEGETABLE TERRINE:

4 baby carrots
4 baby leeks
1 courgette cut into fine strips
1 leek
2g agar agar

MUSTARD MASH:

1lb of Carrolls Heritage Red Duke of York potatoes
1 tsp of dijon mustard
100ml whipping cream
Knob of butter

CHUTNEY JUS:

1 pt of chicken stock
1 measure of Madeira
Sprig of rosemary
1 tsp of apple chutney

METHOD

For the comfit of shoulder: Put all ingredients into a slow cooker and cover with goose fat. Cook for 6 hours when cooked remove meat from bone. Skim off fat and remove vegetables, leaving the stock to reduce by half. Flake meat and bind with reduced stock. Lie out 3 slices of cured ham on cling film, add pork mix down the centre and wrap up to form a sausage like shape and refrigerate.

For the creamed black pudding: Blend black pudding up in a blender then steam till hot and then add Cream.

For the vegetable terrine: Cook baby carrots and baby leeks in salted water till aldente and blanch courgette strips. Retain liquid and reduce to 100ml and add agar agar. Blanch the whole leek then cut down the centre from end to end. Line mould with cling film and then with overlapping leek strips. Add vegetables and compact. Season stock and pour a small amount over vegetables (not too much as this is only to help when slicing the terrine and will melt away when steamed), place in fridge to set. Slice and lightly steam before service.

For the mustard mash: Steam potatoes and pass through sieve. Add other ingredients and bind together.

For the chutney jus: Reduce chicken stock by two thirds, add Madeira and reduce again, add chutney and a knob of butter to finish.

To serve: Cook Noisettes and a slice of the comfit in clarified butter, arrange on plate with other components. Add sauce and a slice of grilled pancetta.

Bamburgh, Northumberland NE70 7EE
Tel: 01668 214581, www.warenhousehotel.co.uk

WILLOW COTTAGE MARMALADE PUDDING WITH CHAIN BRIDGE HEATHER HONEY PARFAIT, AND ORANGE CUSTARD

METHOD

For the marmalade pudding: In a blender mix breadcrumbs, flour and sugar. Melt butter, orange and marmalade in a pan then in a bowl add to breadcrumb mix. Mix in eggs one by one then mix bicarbonate of soda with a little water and add to mixture. Place in moulds and bake in an oven at 160˚C for approx 25min.

For the honey parfait: Put the egg yolks into a bowl. Melt honey in a small pan over a medium heat and bring to the boil. Slowly add the hot honey to the egg yolks and whisk till ribbon stage. In a separate bowl whisk cream till soft peaks. Fold the honey mixture into the cream. Line a terrine with a layer of cling film. Pour in the mixture and freeze.

For the orange custard sauce: Whisk together egg yolks and sugar. Warm cream with orange zest and vanilla pod. Pour into egg mix and then return to the pan, reheat till coating back of a spoon and add Grand Marnier to taste. Strain before service.

INGREDIENTS

Serves 4

MARMALADE PUDDING:

- 150g ground brown bread crumbs
- 25g Self Raising wholemeal flour
- 125g soft brown sugar
- 125g butter
- Zest of one orange
- 175g willow cottage marmalade
- 3 eggs large
- 1tsp bicarbonate of Soda

CHAIN BRIDGE HONEY PARFAIT:

- 2 free-range egg yolks
- 45g heather honey
- 150ml whipping cream

ORANGE CUSTARD SAUCE:

- 4 egg yolks
- 60g castor sugar
- 1/2 vanilla pod
- 400ml whipping cream
- Zest of one orange
- Grand Marnier to taste

Bamburgh, Northumberland NE70 7EE
Tel: 01668 214581, www.warenhousehotel.co.uk

THE WHITE ROOM AT SEAHAM HALL

Lord Byron's Walk, Seaham, County Durham SR7 7AD, Tel: 0191 516 1400, www.tomscompanies.com

TWR
TWR

The award winning White Room Restaurant, led by Michelin-Starred chef Kenny Atkinson is a must for any discerning food connoisseur or critic. The White Room is situated within the indulguent Seaham Hall, a 19 bedroom boutique hotel, set in 37 acres of landscaped gardens. The White Room is understated chic, light and airy with a contemporary feel.

Kenny returned to the North East in August 2008 after achieving his 1st Michelin Star at the Team Restaurant in St Martins, Isle of Scilly. He instantly became a local hero as the accolade was a first for the hotel and island, this secured his entry to an exclusive club, as one of the top 122 chefs in the UK.

Kenny describes his food as Modern British Cuisine, working with the finest fresh local sourced ingredients, constantly changing his menus with the seasons. He worked hard to retain The White Rooms Michelin star, awarded Best Durham Restaurant by the Gourmet Society and in 2009 became the winner of the BBC2 prestigious hit show the Great British Menu, which can be sampled in the White Room throughout the year.

The White Room has two dining areas and can accommodate private dining, as well as the White Room. Kenny oversees and develops menus for many events that are held within the Hotel, from private dinners to sumptuous weddings.

Kenny Atkinson, head chef

Lord Byron's Walk, Seaham, County Durham SR7 7AD
Tel: 0191 516 1400, www.tomscompanies.com

ROLLED TERRINE OF ANJOU QUAIL, HAM HOCK & FOIE GRAS, MARINATED CELERIAC, GRANNY SMITH APPLE & ROASTED HAZELNUTS

METHOD

For the quail terrine: Cook the legs and breasts at 50˚C in a water bath, 2 – 3 hours for the legs and approx 50 minutes for the breasts. When cooked flake & pick the legs and add the fillets & breast to the tray aswell. Rinse the ham hocks under running water for 20 minutes, cover with water and tin foil and braise in the oven for approx 4 hours at 160 degress. When cooked flake the ham hocks and also add to the tray. Pass the stock through a muslin cloth and reduce. Roast the baby onions in a little oil, garlic and thyme until lightly golden. Season and add to the cabbage. Saute the mushrooms whole in olive oil, garlic and thyme, season and when cooked deglaze mushrooms with a little sherry vinegar, add to the tray. Warm the reduced stock and add a splash of truffle arome, madeira and the soaked gelatine leaves, pour over the quail mix. Pan fry the sliced foie gras. Until golden brown, add the parsley to the tray. Correct the season and build the terrine.

For the pickled mushrooms: Quickly saute the mushrooms and thyme and then add the sherry vinegar. Reduce the vinegar. Season and add the hazelnut oil and re-simmer. Set aside. **For the apple puree:** Toss the apples in the lemon juice and place in a pan and add the other ingredients too. Boil until the liquid has absorbed.Blend and pass.

For the marinated celeriac: Mix the lemon juice and the salt into the celeriac and leave for 3 hours. To finish the remoulade squeeze all the juice from the celeriac and add to a bowl, bind with the mayonnaise. Add the mustard and mix in.

For the mushroom powder: Place the dried mushrooms in to a low oven for approx 1 hour at 60˚C. Place into a blender and blitz to a powder, pass through a very fine sieve. **For the roasted hazelnuts:** In a dry pan slowly pan roast the hazel nuts until golden brown. Allow to cool before chopping to a light coarse crumb.

INGREDIENTS

Serves 8

QUAIL TERRINE:

- 16 jumbo quails
- 1 lobe foie gras
- 1 bunch flat leaf parsley
- 200g mushrooms
- 200g baby onions (peeled)
- 6 pints ham stock
- 3 ham hocks
- Ground white pepper
- Truffle arome
- 10 leaves of gelatine (soaked)

PICKLED MUSHROOMS:

- 200g hon shimiji mushrooms
- 2 tbs olive oil
- Sprig thyme
- 6 tbs sherry vinegar
- 200g hazelnut oil

APPLE PUREE:

- 10 granny smith apples
- 75g unsalted butter
- Pinch of salt
- 1 tbs caster sugar
- Juice of 1 lemon
- 150ml water

MARINATED CELERIAC:

- 1 celeriac
- Juice of 3 lemons
- 1 tbs sea salt
- 1 tbs coarse grain mustard
- 3 1/2 tbs mayonnaise

GARNISH:

- 2 discs of quail terrine
- 1 quail egg
- 5 granny smiths
- 8 celery cress
- truffle oil
- 8 hon shimiji mushrooms
- 3 balls of celeriac remoulade
- Pinch of roasted hazel nuts
- 2 smoked pancetta crisps

Lord Byron's Walk, Seaham, County Durham SR7 7AD
Tel: 0191 516 1400, www.tomscompanies.com

ROAST FILLET OF LINE CAUGHT GREY MULLET, BUTTERED BABY SPINACH, CONFIT BABY FENNEL, SWEETYELLOW PEPPER & OLIVE DRESSING

INGREDIENTS

Serves 4

4 fillets grey mullet (175 gm portions, skin on)
3 yellow peppers (skinned and diced)
2 tbs olive oil
1 tsp black olive halves
2 banana shallots (finely chopped)
1 clove garlic (finely chopped)
3 basil and coriander leaves
12 baby fennel bulbs (3 per person)
20g coriander shoots
2 lemons
250g baby spinach

PICKLING SYRUP:

50g water
100g sugar
100 ml white wine vinegar

METHOD

To start: Cook the baby fennel in boiling salted water for approx 2 minutes, remove from the boiling water and plunch into iced water to stop the cooking process and to retain its green colour. When chilled remove the fennel from the water and reserve until needed. Peel the lemon zest and finally cut into thin strips,

To make the pickled lemon: Blanch the zest 3 times in boiling water refreshing in iced water each time, bring the pickling liquor to the boil and simmer for 5 minutes, add the cooked zest bring back to the boil and leave to cool, best left over night for best results.

To make the dressing: Sweat the shallots and garlic in the olive oil without colour, add the julienne of herbs, warm through for 30 seconds before adding the peppers and olives. Season with salt and pepper and finish with a little lemon juice.

To finish the dish: Season the base of the grey mullet with salt and pepper and pan fry slowly skin side down in a non stick pan with a little olive oil. Cook for 6 minutes skin side down and turn over the fish, turn off the heat and allow to the fish to finish cooking with the remaining heat for 2 minutes.

For the spinach: Saute the baby spinach in foaming butter and season, drain spinach onto a cloth. Spoon a neat pile of the spinach into the center of the plate.

For the fennel: Reheat the fennel in boiling water and toss in a little olive oil and seasoning and lay neatly next to the spinach. Warm the pepper and olive dressing and spoon around and over the fennel, garnish with a little pickled lemon zest and coriander shoots, place the crisp grey mullet of top of the spinach and serve.

Lord Byron's Walk, Seaham, County Durham SR7 7AD
Tel: 0191 516 1400, www.tomscompanies.com

RHUBARB JELLY CRUMBLE WITH LEMON FOAM

METHOD

For the jelly: Place the raspberries & chopped rhubarb, sugar, juice into a bowl, cling film and place over a pan of simmering water and leave for 1 hour(do not boil the water). Carefully strain the jus through a fine sieve and muslin cloth. Measure 100 ml of rhubarbjus and add the gelatine and stir in to dissolve. Pour the jelly into martini glasses approx 1/3 full. Chill in the fridge to set.

For the crumble: Rub the butter, flour and sugar to a fine crumb, add the chopped almonds and mix into the crumble mix. Bake at 160 degrees for approx 20 minutes until crisp and light golden brown. Remove from oven and leave to cool.

For the lemon foam: Bring the milk, creamand the peeled lemon zest to the boil and leave to infuse for 30 minutes. Whisk the sugar and eggs together. Reboil the cream and pour onto the eggs and whisk. return to the pan and cook slowly stirring with a wooden spoon until sauce coats the back of the spoon. Pass through a fine sieve, add a few drops of lemon juice to reboost the lemon flavour, add gelatine & chill the lemon sauce over a bowl of ice. When the sauce has chilled pour half full into a gas gun(cream whippers) and inject 2 gas cartridges, return to the fridge until needed.

For the apple sorbet: Toss the apples in the lemon juice and place in the freezer on a flat tray. Bring the water and the sugar to the boil and simmer for 8 minutes, mix in the glugose and the calvados and allow to cool. In a blender blitz the apples slowly adding the stock syrup until a puree appears. Pass through a fine sieve and churn in a ice cream machine.

INGREDIENTS

Serves 4

RHUBARB JELLY:

- 400g rhubarb
- 100g rasberries
- 1/2 lemon - juice only
- 80g caster sugar
- 1 leaves gelatine - soaked in cold water

ALMOND CRUMBLE:

- 100g plain flour
- 50g unsalted butter
- 30g caster sugar
- 75g whole peeled alomnds,chopped
- 10 gm crackle crystals

LEMON FOAM:

- 250g milk
- 250g double cream
- 100g caster sugar
- 8 egg yolks
- 2 lemon zest
- 1/2 gelatine leaf soaked

APPLE SORBET:

- 1 lemon - juice only
- 4 granny smith apples, cored and chopped into 2 cm dices
- 100g sugar
- 200ml water
- 500g glucose syrup
- 25ml calvados

Lord Byron's Walk, Seaham, County Durham SR7 7AD
Tel: 0191 516 1400, www.tomscompanies.com

YOREBRIDGE HOUSE

Bainbridge, Wensleydale, North Yorkshire DL8 3EE, Tel: 01969 650 680, www.yorebridgehouse.co.uk

YOREBRIDGE HOUSE

Nestled in the heart of Wensleydale is Yorebridge House a stunning boutique hotel that has been a real labour of love for its owners Charlotte and Dave Reilly. The eleven bedroom hotel is a stunningly renovated former Victorian school and school master's house, set on the river bank in the beautiful village of Bainbridge set in the Yorkshire Dales National Park. Interior designer Charlotte has crafted showpiece rooms each individually designed with their own subtle style echoing the trends of European design and culture.

Although only open for a relatively short period of time the hotel's restaurant has quickly become a truly talked-about eating destination and is already rated as one of the best in the area.

The Chef is making the most of this rural adventure, making the most of the fine local produce on his doorstep. Menus feature such seasonal produce as game from local shoots as well as traditionally reared meat from farm producers in neighbouring North Yorkshire villages.

With such a wealth of local produce on its doorstep expertly cooked and lovingly served by a truly passionate team Yorebridge House is definitely a destination worth visiting.

Charlotte and Dave Reilly, owners

Bainbridge, Wensleydale, North Yorkshire DL8 3EE
Tel: 01969 650 680, www.yorebridgehouse.co.uk

MONKFISH WITH SERRANO HAM, BABY PLUM TOMATO COMPOTE AND LEMON BASIL JELLY

INGREDIENTS

Serves 2

MONKFISH:

- 500g Monkfish tail (trimmed and cut into 4)
- 4 pieces of Serano ham

JELLY:

- 15 basil leaves
- Juice of 1/2 lemon
- Large pinch of sugar
- 100ml water
- 2 leaves of gelatine
- Salt and pepper (for seasoning)

COMPOTE:

- 1 shallot (finely diced)
- 10 baby plum tomatoes (blanched and peeled)
- 2 cloves garlic (finely diced)
- 2 tbs extra virgin olive oil

METHOD

For the monkfish: Wrap monkfish in ham, wrap in cling film twice and tie, poach for 8 minutes, unwrap and cook in a medium heat pan with oil until golden.

For the jelly: Melt gelatine in lemon and water, add sugar and seasoning, put in liquidizer add basil leaves and blend for 1 minute. Pass through a shinoise and set in a mould.

For the compote: Place all in a small pan, break down on a medium heat around 8 minutes.

Bainbridge, Wensleydale, North Yorkshire DL8 3EE
Tel: 01969 650 680, www.yorebridgehouse.co.uk

ROAST LOIN OF WENSLEYDALE LAMB, BEETROOT PUREE, BRAISED CHICORY, LEMON TYME MADEIRA AND POMMES FONDANT

INGREDIENTS

Serves 1

- 6oz loin of lamb (well trimmed)
- 4 bulbs of beetroot
- 20g butter
- 1 red chicory
- Icing sugar
- 1 spring lemon tyme
- 250 ml chicken stock
- 50 ml maderia
- 1 tbs red wine vinegar
- 1 tblsp sugar
- 1 baking potato
- Salt and pepper

METHOD

For the lamb: Season lamb and seal on a medium heat pan and place on a tray in the oven for 15 minutes at 220˚C.

For the beetroot: Peel beetroot and boil until tender about 25 minutes, drain and leave for 10 minutes. Place in blender until fully pureed. Pass through a drain sieve and heat adding 10 grams of butter and season, once hot serve.

For the fondant: Cut baking potato to desired shape and size, boil in seasoned water until soft, then cook in 10g butter until browned.

For the chicory: Dust in icing sugar and pan fry in olive oil, in a low heat until soft and browned.

For the sauce: Place a pan on a medium heat add vinegar and sugar and reduce until syrup like, add maderia and flambé. Reduce until almost syrup, add stock and lemon tyme reduce until sauce consistency and serve.

Bainbridge, Wensleydale, North Yorkshire DL8 3EE
Tel: 01969 650 680, www.yorebridgehouse.co.uk

YOREBRIDGE HOUSE

CHOCOLATE DELICE WITH SESAME AND ORANGE, LEMON WHITE CHOCOLATE AND GREEN TEA JELLY

METHOD

For the delice: Put egg yolks and cocoa into blender, turn on and slowly add both oils, like a mayonnaise. Melt gelatine in hot water add to mayonnaise mix in blender. Melt chocolate and butter together and add to mayonnaise, then finally add egg whites and orange zest, put into moulds and refridgerate.

For the jelly: Melt chocolate and geletine in milk, add lemon juice strain in a shinoise and pour in a bowl over ice and cool until cream consistancy pour into moulds and set.

INGREDIENTS

Serves 4

DELICE:

300g dark chocolate (preferably valrhone)
25g unsalted butter
½ gelatine leaf
25ml hot water
2 egg yolks
5g cocoa
190ml olive oil
2 tbs sesame oil
5 egg whites (stirred to break down)
Zest of 2 oranges

JELLY:

150ml milk
35g white chocolate
1 leaf gelatine
Juice of ½ lemon

Bainbridge, Wensleydale, North Yorkshire DL8 3EE
Tel: 01969 650 680, www.yorebridgehouse.co.uk

CONTRIBUTORS

BARN ASIA
Waterloo Square, St James Boulevard,
Newcastle upon Tyne NE1 4DN
Tel: 0191 221 1000
www.barnasia.org

BATTLESTEADS HOTEL & RESTAURANT
Wark on Tyne, Hexham,
Northumberland NE48 3LS
Tel: 01434 230209
www.battlesteads.com

THE BAY HORSE
45 The Green, Hurworth, Darlington,
Durham DL2 2AA
Tel: 01325 720 663
www.thebayhorsehurworth.com

BLACK BULL INN
Moulton, Richmond,
North Yorkshire DL10 6QJ
Tel: 01325 377 289, www.blackbullmoulton.com

BLACKFRIARS RESTAURANT
Friars Street, Newcastle NE1 4XN
Tel: 0191 2615945
www.blackfriarsrestaurant.co.uk

THE BLACKSMITHS TABLE
The Green, Washington Old Village
Tyne & Wear NE38 7AB
Tel: 0191 415 1788
www.blacksmithstable.co.uk

BOUCHON BISTRO
4-6 Gilesgate, Hexham
Northumberland NE46 3NJ
Tel: 01434 609 943
www.bouchonbistrot.co.uk

CAFÉ LOWREY
33-35 The Broadway, Darras Hall, Ponteland,
Newcastle Upon Tyne NE20 9PW
Tel: 01661 820 357
www.cafelowrey.co.uk

CASEY'S BRASSERIE
113a High Street, Great Ayton
North Yorkshire TS9 6BW
Tel: 01642 724204

CHAR MAUSAM
Station Road End, Stannington, Morpeth,
Northumberland NE61 6DR
Tel: 01670 789011

THE CHERRY TREE
9 Osborne Road, Jesmond
Newcastle upon Tyne
NE2 2AE Tel: 0191 239 9924
www.thecherrytreejesmond.co.uk

CLOSE HOUSE HOTEL
Bewickes Restaurant
Heddon on the Wall, Newcastle Upon Tyne
NE15 0HT Tel: 01661 852 255
www.closehouse.co.uk

COLMAN'S OF SOUTH SHIELDS
182 - 186 Ocean Road,
South Shields NE33 2JQ
Tel: 0191 456 1202
www.colmansfishandchips.com

CRAB & LOBSTER
Crab Manor Hotel
Dishforth Road, Asenby
Thirsk, North Yorks YO7 3QL
Tel: 01845 577286, www.crabandlobster.co.uk

EPICURUS
Events House, 5 Oslo Close
Tyne Tunnel Trading Estate
North Shields NE29 7SZ
Tel: 0191 270 8540, www.epicurus.co.uk

ESLINGTON VILLA
8 Station Road, Low Fell
Gateshead NE9 6DR
Tel: 0191 487 6017
www.eslingtonvilla.co.uk

THE FEATHERS INN
Hedley On The Hill, Gateshead
NE43 7SW Tel: 01661 843 607
www.thefeathers.net

GREEN'S
13 Bridge Street, Whitby
North Yorkshire YO22 4BG
Tel: 01947 600 284
www.greensofwhitby.com

HORTON GRANGE COUNTRY HOUSE HOTEL & RESTAURANT
Berwick Hill Road, Ponteland
Newcastle upon Tyne
NE13 6BU Tel: 01661 860686
www.hortongrange.co.uk

PAN HAGGERTY
21 Queen Street, Newcastle
NE1 3UG Tel: 0191 221 0904
www.panhaggerty.com

FILINI
Framwellgate Waterside, City of Durham,
County Durham DH1 5TL
Tel: 191 372 7200
www.radissonblu.co.uk/hotel-durham

THE RAT INN
Anick, Hexham, Northumberland
NE46 4LN Tel: 01434 602814
www.theratinn.com

RIVERSIDE RESTAURANT
Bridge End, Barnard Castle
Co. Durham DL12 9BE
Tel: 01833 637 576
www.riverside-restaurant.co.uk

SACHINS
Forth Banks, Newcastle upon Tyne NE1 3SG
Tel: 0191 232 4660 / 261 9035
www.sachins.co.uk

SIX RESTAURANT AT BALTIC
BALTIC Centre for Contemporary Art
South Shore Road, Gateshead
NE8 3BA Tel: 0191 440 4948
www.sixbaltic.com

THE STABLES
The Granary, Wynyard Village
TS22 5QQ
Tel: 01740 644 074

STARTER & PUDS
2-6 Shakespeare Street
Newcastle Upon Tyne NE1 6AQ
Tel:0191 233 2515
www.startersandpuds.co.uk

THE WAITING ROOM
9 Station Rd, Eaglescliffe
Stockton-On-Tees, Cleveland TS16 0BU
Tel: 01642 780465
www.the-waiting-room.co.uk

WAREN HOUSE HOTEL
Bamburgh, Northumberland NE70 7EE
Tel: 01668 214581
www.warenhousehotel.co.uk

THE WHITE ROOM AT SEAHAM HALL
Lord Byron's Walk, Seaham
County Durham SR7 7AD
Tel: 0191 516 1400
www.tomscompanies.com

YOREBRIDGE HOUSE
Bainbridge, Wensleydale
North Yorkshire DL8 3EE
Tel: 01969 650 680
www.yorebridgehouse.co.uk

1 prix fix s
1 POTTED CRAB
1 CHICKEN PIE
1 GNOCCHI PARISI
1 prix fix main A
1 prix fix main B
1 DUCK FAT CHIPS
MIXED SALAD

1 PEA & HA
2 MUSSELS
1 CHICKEN PIE
2 BELLY PORK
2 POMME PUREE
1 FINE BEANS
1 ROAST CARROTS
1 SPRING CABBAGE

1 CRAYF
1 CHICKEN